ACKNOWLEDGEMENTS

The Committee for Anglophone Social Action (CASA) would like to acknowledge the financial assistance provided by the Department of Canadian Heritage for the preparation and publishing of this book, under the *Community Life* component of the *Development of Official-Language Communities* program.

Thank you to the Gilker family for allowing us to use the artwork on the front cover. The portrait of Earlene M. Wark Gilker was done by Maciek Szczerbowski, who works in stop motion animation in Montreal and Toronto. The Gaspé is a very special place for Maciek. The circumstances surrounding the production of this particular piece of art are certainly another story worth hearing!

Sincere thanks and appreciation goes out to the many volunteers and staff who worked on completing this project.

Most importantly, we would like to express our gratefulness to our storytellers, both young and old, for allowing us a personal glimpse into our rich Gaspesian history.

A Brief History of the Gaspé Peninsula

'The Birthplace of Canada'

The Mi'kmaq occupied this land centuries before the first Europeans arrived and were probably the first Native Americans to have regular contact with Europeans. This may have occurred as early as the 11th century with the early Viking settlements on the coast of North America. The Mi'kmaq were skilled hunter-gatherers, attuned to the shifting, seasonal resources of the area and were noted for their fishing skills and their distinctive birch bark canoes that were capable of crossing open water.

1534   Jacques Cartier finds a safe harbour in Gaspé Bay and erects a cross, claiming the land for King Francis I of France. This marks the beginning of French presence in North America.

1750's   Channel Island immigrants begin to arrive in the Gaspé.

1758   The British raid the Gaspé Coast under General James Wolfe and take command of many French settlements in the region.

1760   Acadian refugees begin to arrive in the Restigouche area and gradually move eastward to Chaleur Bay settling mainly in Tracadieche (Carleton), Bonaventure and Paspebiac.
The British win the Battle of the Restigouche, the last naval battle between France and England for possession of the North American continent.

1760's   Fishermen from Newfoundland, Ireland and the American Colonies begin to settle in the Percé area and inhabit Bonaventure Island.

1763   The Gaspé officially becomes a part of the 'province of Quebec.'

1767   Charles Robin, a native of the Channel Islands arrives in Paspebiac and sets up a fishing establishment, eventually building a monopoly.

1770   Shoolbred & Smith (British businessmen) receive a large grant of land in Restigouche and set up a salmon exporting business, bringing in a number of men from Aberdeen, Scotland to work as fishermen, coopers and packers. Pirates from the American Colonies attack and destroy the operation a few years later and the Scottish settlers move eastward along the Coast.

1777   One of the first recorded sailing vessels to be built on the Gaspé Coast was constructed in the Chaleur Bay area by Louis Vachon. From that date until 1925 there were at least 600 sailing ships built on the Coast. This estimate does not include the many whaling ships built in and around the Gaspé Bay area during the 18th and 19th centuries.

1784   Following the end of the Revolutionary War, the Loyalists – British Americans who had remained loyal to the British Crown after the 13 American colonies gained their independence – arrive and establish farming communities mainly in New Carlisle, New Richmond and Douglastown.

1796   The first post office is established in Carleton.

1816   A famine strikes the Gaspé Coast in the winter of 1816-1817.

1820   Scottish settlers begin to make their way to the Coast, often sailing back to Canada on privately owned vessels that had carried cargos of lumber, fish and furs to Great Britain.

1825   A smaller group of settlers come to the Coast after losing their homes and livelihood in the Great Miramichi Fire, which destroyed thousands of acres of woodland and all homes and buildings on the north side of the Miramichi River for hundreds of miles in all directions.

1840   Waves of Irish immigrants arrive in the 1840's when potato crops failed in Ireland.

1847   Irish brig *Carricks* carrying Irish immigrants to Montreal, is destroyed during a storm at Cap des Rosiers, with a loss of 120 lives. Some passengers survive and settle in the area.

1850   All communities make up a total population of less than 20,000, of whom half are English-speaking. The population is primarily located in the Chaleur Bay area.

1906   The Bonaventure and Gaspé Telephone Company is founded.

1911   The railway from Matapedia to Gaspé is completed.

1914   On October 3, the 1st Division of the Canadian Expeditionary Force sails from Gaspé Harbour bound for Europe. It is the largest convoy to ever sail from Canadian waters, consisting of 32 transport ships and 7 warships. The vessels carry a total of 30,617 officers and soldiers and 7,679 horses, as well as other equipment for the war effort.

1920   In the late 1920's, a road (Highway 132) is finally completed, encircling the entire peninsula.

1922   René Lévesque is born in Campbellton, NB to parents living in New Carlisle, where René grows up. He later becomes a war correspondent and then enters politics, becoming premier of Quebec for the Parti Québécois.

1940   Gaspé Bay becomes a strategic spot for the Ministry of National Defence during World War II.

1942   The Battle of the Gulf of St. Lawrence takes place. German U-boats sink 23 ships between 1942 and 1944. The HMCS Fort Ramsay naval base is inaugurated in Gaspé. A German spy, Werner von Janowski, is captured in New Carlisle and later used as a double agent in Canada and Britain.

1951   Roads are first opened in the winter.

1954   Wilbert Coffin is found guilty of the murder of three American hunters and sentenced to death by hanging. Coffin is hanged at Montreal's Bordeaux prison on February 10, 1956.

1955   Noranda begins mining copper ore in the Gaspé, starting a period of growth and employment for the new town of Murdochville.

1970   The establishment of Forillon National Park in 1970 was preceded by the confiscation of property and expropriation of several families that had settled within the boundaries of the eventual park. Families were forced to re-settle in the surrounding areas.

1971   Bonaventure Island is purchased by the Quebec government who expropriate the entire island. Parc national de l'Île-Bonaventure-et-du-Rocher-Percé is created in 1985 and is now one of the largest bird sanctuaries in the world.

Introduction

CASA was created in 1975 to respond to the needs of the English-speaking community of the Gaspé Coast. For years, CASA has worked to promote the importance of our culture, history and heritage.

It is our great pleasure to offer you the first volume of *Once Upon a Time in the Gaspé.*

This undertaking began when high school students and volunteers interviewed Gaspesian seniors and captured their stories on film.

In 2004, seniors were revisited and new interviews conducted. Elementary and secondary students competed in the *Once Upon a Time* storytelling contest. Students from several schools interviewed neighbours and relatives and wrote stories on what life was like for them years ago on the Gaspé Coast.

Unfortunately, we could not include all of the wonderful stories which were received. However, a second volume of Gaspesian stories will be published in the future to include many more Gaspesian experiences, legends, tales, yarns and anecdotes.

We hope that this book will inspire you to share your memories with family, friends and neighbours and to sit with parents and grandparents, and listen to their wonderful stories.

And yes, Draven, your book is finally ready.

Kim Harrison
Executive Director
CASA

Winter Fun

The Frozen Pig Story

As told by Gerard Poirier

Gerard was born in Fauvel in 1918 and raised in New Carlisle. He served in the Air Force from 1940 to 1945 and worked at CN Rail for 35 years. Gerard is an avid storyteller and enjoys reading and writing. He resides in New Carlisle with his wife Marion.

There were three men who lived in New Carlisle back in the early 1920's and 1930's who were known as the scallywags of New Carlisle. They were always up to some sort of tricks or badness. Frank Weary, Elmer Astels and Smithy Astels would be out on the town in the dead of winter, just like they were each and every night of the year.

Elmer and Smithy would often get home around midnight and, to keep from freezing to death in the house that they lived in, they often shared the same bed. On this particular night Elmer came home before Smithy. It just so happened that they had killed a pig that day and had it standing up frozen in the corner of the room.

Well, Elmer, being Elmer, decided to put it in the bed and cover it up as though it was him lying there. When Smithy got home and climbed into bed he could feel the cold next to him. He touched the pig and said, 'Elmer, Elmer are you okay?' He was sure that Elmer was dead and frozen solid beside him in bed. It took a while for him to realize that it wasn't Elmer. Meanwhile, Elmer was standing behind the door, laughing his head off. Those two were always up to some kind of badness like this all the time.

Our Rink

As told by Richard Hunt

Richard was born in Pabos in 1933 and worked as a crane operator for the Gaspesia Company for 25 years until retirement. He loves mechanics and working on motors and is a wonderful storyteller and fiddler. He still resides in Chandler.

When the ice was thick enough to haul wood across, the lake would become our rink for skating and hockey. We used to play hockey from the minute we cleared the snow off to the minute the ice started to crack and melt. We had to have a rink for the boys and a rink for the girls because the girls wanted nothing to do with hockey. All they did was complain about us playing hockey all the time, so we made them a rink of their own where they could skate and we could play hockey in peace.

We used to make up hockey teams and set up a little game between friends. We'd cut a slice of birch off a tree and that would be our hockey puck. The hockey sticks would be made out of alders, curved up a bit at the bottom to make 'em shoot better. We had a team, although I don't remember everyone's names. There was Leonard Murphy, my brother Stanley,

Glen Murphy, Russell, Miles Murray and Ray Hunt to name a few. Ray was the goalie. With no hockey stick, Ray would use his scraper to both clear the ice and to guard the goal. He used old catalogues and cardboard boxes tied to his legs for pads. We'd use boots to mark the goals and some of us would cheat and put the boots closer together.

I remember one time when we lost the puck. It flew down the rink and 'plop', right into the water; it was gone. There were always horses and oxen crossing the lake so we managed to find some horse manure – frozen of course. We used that manure patty as a puck for the rest of the day. It was frozen solid which made it a little difficult to play with. In the middle of the game, one of the little guys made a break and went flying down the ice with the manure puck heading straight towards his father, who was the goalie for the other team.

His father, padded with catalogues from head to toe, yelled out, 'Don't shoot! Don't shoot!'

That little guy drew back and hit that manure with all his might sending it flying through the air, knocking the smoking pipe out of his father's mouth. His father was furious. I wouldn't want to get a face full of horse manure either.

'I told you not to shoot!' he shouted. The little guy started running for his life and his father took off after him. Neither of them was very good at running with skates on and they kept falling down. Anyways, the game ended there. We felt sorry for the little guy, but it was one of the funniest things we ever saw. Those were the good times.

The Victrola

As told by Elton Hayes

Born in Shigawake in 1929, Elton worked as a dairy farmer. He received l'Ordre de Merit Agricole in 1989. Upon retirement he began to breed colts for racetracks. He has worked for the Shigawake Municipality for 45 years.

When I was about 5 years old my father had a skating rink in the lower field near our house. Every year he would take the horses, go back to the spring behind our house and fill up a great big 90-gallon molasses puncheon. He had the horses shoed so that they could walk out on the ice. Once he filled the puncheon with water, he would put a hole in the bottom so that the water would come out slowly and it would flood the ice. In the evening, he would hang gasoline lanterns up on poles and he would play an old Victrola with Strauss music so that we could skate to the music. But we couldn't play hockey at night, because the lights weren't strong enough to see the puck.

Little Pete

As told by Ivan and Elsie Patterson

Ivan Patterson, a World War II veteran, was born in Sandy Beach in 1922. His wife, Elsie, was born in York in 1918. The couple continues to reside in Gaspé.

Jerry and Leo Beattie with Peninsula in the foreground.

One time when little Pete was out sliding with the neighbours, his little toboggan hit ice and wouldn't stop. He wasn't old enough to know to jump off and the toboggan went onto the road and kept going. Well, he slid right under a truck and came out the back end, split the ski-doo suit right in half. That was one of his nine lives.

Winter Bells

As told by Elton Hayes

When we got to be teenagers, we took the girls out with the horse and sleigh. We had lazy backs, which were made with boards on the sides. The back was slanted like an easy chair and you filled it with hay. You tucked your girl in beside you, covered up with buffalo robes, put your arm around her and you went to the skating rink.

There were always four or five horses in Hopetown and we would all meet up and drive around at the same time. It was so much fun. Someone would push two or three people off the front sleigh and they'd get on the sleigh behind, and push someone off there. Before you knew it, the sleigh in the back would have about fifteen people on it and we'd have to stop, because the horse couldn't keep up with the rest. We had more fun coming and going than anything else. Everyone had bells on their horses and each bell gave off a unique sound. Some of them were coarse bells, some of them soft bells and some of them chanting bells. The bells let other people know that they had to make room on the road for another horse and sleigh.

Pork Barrel Skis

As told by Richard Hunt

Little Jimmy Gillis on skis

My Uncle Pete was so good-hearted. You see, he always had time for us kids, he was never too busy. He lived in the old building near Beaubassin and was liked by all the children for miles around. He had kids of his own and yet he took the time to play with us. I remember once he helped me make a pair of skis from the hoops of my father's pork barrel.

We used the steel from the sides of the pork barrel to make the skis and then we used a piece of raw hide to go over them to make the bindings. Then, we cut little alders of spruce and peeled them and made the poles. When the springtime came, my father asked where his pork barrel was and I never said a word, neither would my Uncle Pete. I never told my father that I had used the pork barrel to make my skis. He was a very strict man and he would not have taken lightly to my using his pork barrel for my enjoyment.

The Fur Coat

Ted Syvret, Age 11, Gaspé Elementary School

Once upon a time my grandfather told me that his grandmother was sick and needed a doctor. Where they lived in Forillon Park, the roads weren't open all winter, so they had to come to Gaspé with a horse and sleigh and cross on the ice in a blizzard to get Doctor Fortier. Then they had to bring him back. He was so cold that night my grandfather said they got together and collected money to buy the doctor a fur coat. He was young and had just become a doctor. 'We really appreciated what that doctor did for us,' he said.

The Glo' Worms

Derek Harrison, Age 10, New Richmond High School

Once upon a time in the Gaspé, my granny played hockey in Cascapedia. It was in 1950 when she started to play. Her team was called the 'Glo' Worms'. The coach was Mr. J. A. Campbell. They travelled to New Richmond and Caplan in a truck owned by Luke Geraghty with a canvas covered box and two wooden benches. They had a great time singing 'Glo' Little Glo' Worms'.

Granny said there was one girl from New Richmond that they were all afraid of: she liked to fight. Her name was Yvonne MacIntyre. I was shocked to hear Granny tell me they never wore helmets or any other hockey gear, just skates and a hockey stick.

She always played outside, where it was freezing cold, but said she had lots of fun.

ELECTIONS IN THE GASPÉ

The One and Only Sid Maloney

As told by Alexandre Cyr

As Liberal MP, Alexandre Cyr won the Gaspé riding in 1963, was defeated in 1965, re-elected in 1968 and then served continuously until 1984. In the tumultuous mid-60's, he became a prominent supporter of the new Canadian flag and following its adoption, composed the 'Pledge of Allegiance to the Canadian Flag.' He currently resides in Chandler.

Alexandre Cyr and Prime Minister Trudeau in Ottawa

Electoral campaigns along the Gaspé Coast were always one of a kind, especially on Bonaventure Island. Sidney Maloney was the federal Liberal organizer, the returning officer, the elections clerk – he did it all!

In 1949 there were around 30 voters on the island and most of them were English-speaking. Sid knew that everybody on the island was voting for the Liberals, because most of the time they were voting right in front of him.

He personally knew everyone on the voting list and if someone was sick or couldn't leave their house, he would just take the ballot box and go right to them. He'd visit the old ladies and the old men who couldn't get out and get their votes.

By ten in the morning everyone would be done voting and Sid would be back in Percé an hour later with the box of votes to hand over results, which in '49 was 28 Liberals and one Conservative. As the years went on, it went down to fifteen Liberals and one Conservative and finally, in 1971 before the island was declared a historical park, eight Liberals and one Conservative.

One day, Sid was up in Ottawa telling all this to Prime Minister Trudeau. I remember it well; I was a member of parliament at the time and I was there. Mr. Trudeau asked him, 'So do you know who was voting Conservative all this time?'

'It was me!' Sid exclaimed.

Sid Maloney, our Liberal officer, the Liberal organizer, told our Liberal prime minister, 'I'm the one that voted Conservative.' Nobody knew.

Mr. Trudeau, quite surprised, said, 'It would have been nice if you had been able to report the results as 29 voters, 29 Liberal votes.'

Sid replied, 'Oh no, Mr. Trudeau! I could never do that! Never! In case the government changed, there would always be a Tory and a Conservative on the island to ask the government to repair the wharf!'

A Terrible Piece of Work

As told by Raymond Hunt

*Raymond was born in Chandler West in 1918. He was a 'poler',
which was a specialized job when driving logs down a river.
He also worked as a forest ranger, reporting any fires seen from
his tower, and worked as a fishing guide and warden.*

I used to be the manager for every election. I would work
at the polls on Election Day. My job was to sit there and mark
off all the names of people who had voted, then count the
votes to see who had won. The first year we had elections
there were some awful fights! Oh, it was a terrible piece of
work trying to hold an election in those days. There were
always some people who would get drunk and their argu-
ments would quickly turn into brawls. It's sure not like that
anymore.

Election Time Fights

As told by Louis Brochet

*Louis was born in Grand River in 1918. He was the captain of
a tourist boat around Bonaventure Island and was also a game
warden for a period of time. Louis has kept busy with his cabin
rental business. He has also done his share of farming, cod fishing
and motor boating. He resides in Percé.*

Politics back in the day were certainly not as sophisticated
as they are today. Nomination day was held in Percé at the
courthouse, and both parties would be together for nomina-
tions at the same time. Back in the 1930's, there was a lot of
contraband liquor floating around, and it really didn't help to
keep matters quiet or to keep tempers under control. There
were always a few bloody noses around election time. People
learned later on that most politicians aren't worth fighting
for, but they sure didn't realize it then. It was pretty rough
around election time.

School Days

Teacher from the Townships

As told by Earlene Gilker

Earlene was born January 1, 1914 in Leeds. She lived in Kinnear's Mills, Megantic County, before settling in New Carlisle as a school teacher for 34 years. Her portrait is featured on the cover of this book.

I was born and raised in the Eastern Townships and went to school at Macdonald College in St. Anne de Bellevue. Teachers were a dime a dozen or so in my graduating class. Times were hard and finding a teaching job wasn't an easy task; there were many more teachers than there were positions available.

I'd been out of college three years when I applied for a position in New Carlisle. When I first arrived in New Carlisle in 1937 I taught grade 3, then grade 8 and finally high school. I used to board at Mrs. George Gilker's. She ran an eight-room boarding house.

I remember my first Sunday in New Carlisle well. I went for a walk down on the beach and found some of those famous razor blade shells. I was so proud of my find, having been raised in the Eastern Townships where we didn't even have a beach to walk on, never mind shells to find. After speaking to Mrs. Gilker's son, Geordie, I was told that I had not found razor blade shells, but I had found something better – mermaid's fingernails! I had such fun boarding there. I even ended up marrying Geordie's cousin, Jim Gilker.

When the war started, Jim wanted to be patriotic and join the forces, to do his part. He had his heart set on joining the Air Force and went to the recruiting offices in Quebec City. They wouldn't take him because he had enlarged tonsils; he'd have to have them removed. Well, my husband, being the man that he was, thanked them and crossed the street to the Army recruiting offices and signed up. They took him right then and there, tonsils and all. He died with those very same tonsils many years later.

During the war, I taught in several mining towns located throughout northern Quebec such as Malarctic and Rapide Blanc. To keep busy after Jim enlisted, I decided to take up shooting and even won awards as a Dominion Markswoman.

During my teaching years, I can't say that I ever had any real trouble with any of my students. In my day, teachers were forbidden to discuss politics in school and religion was also taboo, unlike today where the liveliest discussions on any given subject take place. How times have changed.

They used to heat the school with wood. During the Depression, the taxpayers couldn't always afford to pay taxes so they would bring in wood – four-foot lengths – to fill the great big furnace in the basement. Mr. Will Flowers, the janitor, even had to spend evenings at school stoking the fires through the night when it was very cold outside.

There being no such thing as snow blowers, we had to wade through the very deep cold snow to go to school. I think we were more accustomed to rough weather back then, it happened regularly in those days. Unlike today, the school rarely closed due to weather conditions, but we did wonder sometimes if we would even get to school!

Those who lived within a mile of the school walked, any further than that and you were picked up by what they called 'hacks'. A hack was all covered in, like a wooden cupboard. In the fall and spring it was drawn on wheels by horses, but during the winters it had sleigh runners underneath it.

I would definitely say that life in the Gaspé was more difficult than what I was used to, but I taught here for 34 years and I loved every minute of it. I'd even miss those children when I was back in the Townships for the summer.

The Hack

Hannah Robinson, Age 8, Shigawake-Port Daniel School

Once upon a time in the Gaspé my great-granddad, Aubrey McRae, used to pick up the students and take them to Hopetown School by horse and hack. My great-granddad made the trailer (what the kids called the hack) from the frame of an old truck. My great-grandma made seats for the children to sit on and they sat two-by-two. Two horses, Suze and Fred, hauled the trailer. My great-granddad had about twenty students use the hack everyday and it took him about two hours to pick them all up. There was a lot of snow and they did not open the roads with ploughs so my great-granddad could not take the children all winter.

My other great-grandpa, Ruben McRae, would take over with his snowmobile. Before great-grandpa Ruben would take over, when the roads were slippery, my great-granddad McRae would ask the students to get off the hack and walk up the River Hill behind the horses. When I asked my grandma, Dora Robinson (who was a student that drove on the hack) about the times that she went to school by horse, she smiled and said that was her favourite way to go to school.

My great-granddad drove the hack for about five years, then he continued to pick up students by bus for another nineteen years.

The One-Room Schoolhouse

Ryan O'Connor, Age 8, Gaspé Elementary School

My grandmother and grandfather both went to school in one-room schoolhouses. There was one teacher for seven grades and 20 or 30 students in one room. They walked a mile to school. Many children packed their lunch of home-made bread and molasses in a newspaper.

At my grandmother's school a boy would light the stove every morning to keep the school warm. One day a girl went too close and her apron caught on fire. She was lucky to put the fire out.

Another day a boy put a pencil in his mouth. Parents would cut one pencil into three pieces to save money. One pencil could then be used by three children in the same family. On that day, he chewed on his pencil and nearly choked. He was lucky and it flew across the room.

The inspector would come to school once a year to test the students. The teacher gave my grandmother and her friend page 37 in French to practise for a whole month. They knew it very well. On the day the inspector came, he gave them a different page to read. They did not know any of the words and they started to laugh. They both failed.

Sometimes the students got in trouble. They would get a good spanking. One day my grandfather and his friends put a pail of water on top of the door. The teacher opened the door and got all soaking wet. Some of them got a spanking with her leather strap.

At my grandmother's school, the students decided to climb up and hide in the attic of the school. A girl was afraid and started to cry half way up. Granny was holding the door and was told not to help the bad children. Some of them also got a spanking with the teacher's leather strap. It was very flexible!

My grandmother went to school in Haldimand and my grandfather went to school in Point St. Peter. They met many years later.

War Stories

Germans Sighted on Gaspé Coast

As told by Eva Robertson

Eva was born in New Richmond in 1924. Her first job, at age 14, was working at Campbell's Inn. She also worked in a bake shop wrapping bread that was sent by train to soldiers in Gaspé. In addition to working at Annett's Hotel, she worked for the Department of Tourism, Fish and Game for eighteen seasons. She now resides at the New Richmond Manor where she spends her spare time painting, and knitting bonnets, booties and mittens for premature babies.

My father was a lighthouse keeper from 1925 to 1940. We all had chores as children and it was my responsibility to keep the globe on the lighthouse lantern clean so that the boats could see the light coming in to the harbour and not go aground. Every morning I would go down to the lighthouse with my dad.

There is one morning in particular that I will never forget. My father and I were at the lighthouse and noticed an unusual looking fishing boat at the wharf. My father was a man of very few words, but that morning he commented on something not quite right about that boat. A gentleman came off the boat and approached my father. I continued to clean the glass lamp and watched as my father spoke with the stranger. He told my father that the fishing boat was from Germany and they were here fishing scallops.

That evening, my grandfather dropped by to visit and my father told him what we had seen in the harbour and how he thought the entire situation very strange. The crew had no nets and no crates, yet they said that they were scallop fishermen. My father suggested that this boat was up to no good in our harbour.

The next day we went down to the lighthouse, and the gentleman approached my father again and asked him if we had any buttermilk. My father told him that we churned our own and that he would bring him some the following day. For the next few days we took them buttermilk, but one day when we got to the lighthouse the stranger's boat was nowhere to be seen! Father later told grandfather that he had suspected that they were sounding the depth of the harbour for submarines. We did see the boat out in the bay for the next little while, but eventually the boat disappeared from there as well.

Several years later, I applied for and got a job at Annett's Hotel in New Carlisle. This is where I eventually met young Earl Annett, the owner's son. He recounted this story of how a German spy by the name of Werner Alfred Waldemar von Janowski came ashore in a rubber dinghy in November of 1942 and was caught in New Carlisle.

He showed me where the German spy had spent the night and had eaten his breakfast. He told me that Mrs. Annett was the one who had initially mentioned a very unusual smell about the man. She said it reminded her of the smell when her husband had worked on the lake boats. It was a very strong smell of diesel that was not easily mistaken. Apparently, the spy had taken off his smelly clothes and stuffed them under the tub in his hotel room; but a smell like that lingers for a very long time and that is why Mrs. Annett was able to detect it when she passed the room. That smell was what made her suspicious.

What's more, when the man went to pay for his room, he said that he had just arrived from Gaspé on a bus and that he would be on his way to Montreal on the train the next day. Well, Earl knew that there had been no bus from Gaspé and he found this to be rather sketchy. The man then lit a cigarette and dropped his matches; Earl immediately noted that they were not recognizable matches. They had foreign writing on them which Earl did not recognize. He also noticed that the man was wearing a suit that was definitely not Canadian cut. He said that it was obviously tailored somewhere else.

The minute that the man left for the train station, Earl contacted the police to inform them of his apprehensions. He told them about this shady character that had just spent the night at his hotel. The police laughed and said that there was no spy in New Carlisle. Earl had such a strong suspicion, though, that he went directly to the police at the Maison Blanche and rallied them to go to Bonaventure and get on the train to check out his suspicions. He told the police that if they would not do this, then he would personally make a citizen's arrest. This was how strongly he believed that something was going on.

Sure enough, when the police got on the train and asked Earl to identify the man, the German man surrendered without any kind of fight or retaliation, and asked the police to take him to the beach so that he could show them his uniform.

He wanted to be arrested as a prisoner of war rather than as a German spy. The police took him to the beach where he dug up his uniform and put it on. He then proceeded to salute towards the bay and told the police that if the German submarines in the bay knew what was happening to him, they would blow up the Gaspé. This German spy later worked as a double agent in Canada and Britain.

It's something that when I was a little girl helping my father out at the lighthouse I got to see a German spy boat and then when I was a young working woman, I worked at a hotel where the German spy had been caught!

Women at War

As told by Marion Poirier

Marion was born in Saskatchewan in 1922. After serving in the Air Force, she married Gerard Poirier and moved to New Carlisle where they started their family. Marion is very artistic and her hand-made quilts have sold internationally. Role models like Marion blazed a path for women today.

Marion Poirier in uniform

As a young woman in British Columbia, I was working in a five and ten-cent store earning twelve dollars a month. There weren't many jobs for women, besides getting married that is, and after having two sisters who married before the age of eighteen, I was determined I was not going to do the same!

There was a very narrow road for women back then, I can still hear my father saying, 'get married and look after your husband.' At the time, posters were plastered all over the city enticing young men and women to join the Army, Navy and Air Force. I went ahead and enlisted without telling my parents. I guess you could say I was a rebel! Three months later I received a letter and was called into service.

Scared and alone, I went down to the train station with my little cardboard suitcase; I just knew I had to go through with it! I met up with some other girls on the train who were also joining the service and ended up going through the war with those very girls!

When we first arrived on the base in Mont Joli, some of the men that were stationed there thought that we were there for their pleasure. They didn't realize what a group of innocent, decent girls we were. The very first night that we were on the base, there was a party and the guys came in from the hangers, all greasy and dirty (and that would describe exactly how they were acting, too!). We took one look at them and walked out of the party. It took a while before they realized that we were there to work in the Air Force, just the same as they were. Sometimes, you had to put up with nasty comments just because you were a girl in uniform.

We spent two years stationed in Mont Joli before going overseas. In February 1944, we landed in Scotland and then headed south to London. I stayed in an apartment in London where I started working for the medical board. The job was very difficult because they would be bringing in young boys with burned faces from bomber and fighter plane crashes.

I remember one incident; I was sitting at my station when an attendant brought in a young man and left him sitting in the waiting area. I looked straight at him and paused. I could tell that he'd been through rounds of plastic surgery and he still had a long way to go. His eyes were only little slits in his face. His hands were gone ... I guess he saw the expression of sorrow on my face and he started to weep. He was just a kid.

I immediately went over to him and put my arm around him and there we sobbed together. Through tears, he managed to tell me that he was a gunner. He told me that he had a girlfriend and was scared that there was no way she would ever have him back, looking like this. The young man was only 19. That moment is seared in my memory forever.

After that incident, I asked to be transferred to the statistics branch where I stayed until the end of the war.

It was a terrible shock when I got back to Canada and we all went our separate ways. We had become our own little family during the war. My own family remained in Canada's west, my Air Force family went their separate ways, and I came to New Carlisle. What surprised us the most afterward was that people back home thought that we women were safe in London and out of harm's way the entire time. They had no idea that London was a war zone. Little did they know that we were there, knocked out of our beds with concussions, hearing the sirens and then the noise of the V2 rockets, not knowing if the next explosion would be 'the one'.

Unfortunately, many people still don't realize what a service the women in uniform did for our country. We truly opened up the world for women today, all 50,000 of us. Many women served this country and gave their lives doing so.

A POW in World War II

As told by Joseph Arnold Hunt

Joseph was born in Pabos in 1910, the oldest boy in a family of sixteen children. One fall, after finishing school, he put a packsack on his back, jumped a boxcar and went to Gaspé where he found work cutting pulp. He then joined the Army and served in the Royal Rifles of Canada.

During World War II, I was a member of the Royal Rifles of Canada. My number was E29864, and my company was D Company. We were captured in Hong Kong and taken prisoner by the Japanese. We were kept at Shamshuipo Camp for a long time, before being taken to Niigata, Japan to work in a slave labour camp.

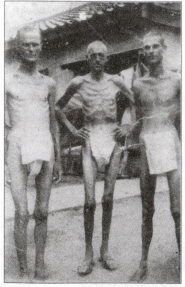

Unidentified Prisoners of War

I was sent to work in the foundries where they used iron; it's called pig iron in English. There was a long pole, about maybe fifteen or sixteen feet long, with a cup at the end of it. We'd shove it on a piece of pig iron that was in the furnace and then back it out and a trolley would bring it to the press. Sometimes we'd back away from the furnace because it was so hot, and the guard would scream, 'Work! Work!' His face was murderous. We didn't have protective clothing to work there, just the shorts and shirts we had in the Army.

Beatings were common at Niigata – I saw other fellows get beaten up several times. When they were beating you, you'd look up from the ground and there would be a fellow in the corner, always just waiting for you to do something, to resist their punishment.

After a couple of beatings, they put me on a little stoker where they used to make bolts. I would put the coal in the stoker, then put the bolts in and rend them and take them out. Another fellow there would thread them.

One morning a little Jap just about my size came in saying, 'Good morning, good morning!'

I said, 'Good morning, sir. You speak English?'

'Yes,' he said, 'Me go school in Calgary.'

'Yeah,' I said, 'You come here on visit?' And he said that no, they had sent him there to work.

One day we were working and he said to me, 'Me and you wrestle.'

'Oh Jesus. Oh no, no wrestle.' I said, but the old foreman told us that if there was no work, we could wrestle. So we did that for maybe three or four months, until one day I came in and picked him up and threw him over my shoulder into the coal bin.

He got out and said, 'That's good, you learn good. Come again and try again.'

But I never got a chance because the next thing I felt a big iron rod hit me across the back. The guards were beating me. I fell to my knees and the little fellow went over to tell them it was okay, that we were wrestling. But they slapped him across the face and made him cry. I felt sorry for him, but when I went to get up they gave me another hit across the back. I fell down and two guards came and beat me up. I had a cut across my face and I was bleeding down my nose. Each of the Japanese guards took their turn beating me up, and then I asked to go to the banjo (bathroom). I went in there and I washed all the blood off and I said to myself, 'This is my last day. If they come back after me, I'm taking the shovel and I'm going to slash them across the face with it. Then I'm going to take their rifles and I'm shooting until they're empty.' I was so angry.

What helped me last through all of those beatings was something I remembered from a fellow who had taught me how to box – Joe Ward. He told me that whenever you see a blow coming towards you, never keep your head solid, let your head go with the blow.

A few hours later the sirens started ringing. The Americans had opened fire on us. So everybody ran out and went underground to hide from the guns. It wasn't so nice under there – dark and cold. When we came out from the underground to work again, we were there only about twenty minutes before the sirens started to ring again. The Japs had a big boat at sea with an ammunition factory on it and the Americans had dropped a bomb on the boat.

The next day was announced as a rest day. And then the day after that, too. So by the third day we were wondering what was going on with the Japs that they weren't making us work. We figured it had something to do with the attack by the Americans. We were outside eating our little bit of daily rice when we saw a plane coming. It kept flying lower and lower, and then it started dropping pamphlets. One fell just in behind the camp, so I went and picked it up and brought it to Captain Price. He was inside reading it for about an hour and then he came outside to talk to us.

'Well boys,' he said, 'I don't want you to go wild. I want you to be calm and keep quiet. The war is officially over; we don't want to start another one. Try and keep calm. What we're going to do, is try and get some paint, and we're going to go up on that roof there, and paint P.O.W. – Prisoner of War. Make the letters as big as you can so they can see them when they come back.'

So myself and another fellow were just about done painting the roof when we saw another plane coming. I crawled over to the side of the roof because I thought he was going to land on us, he was flying so low. Anyway, he started dropping stuff – big barrels and parachutes. One fell in the camp on the other side of us where we used to sleep. Corporal Dow and Jim Darva were in there talking to one another and the barrel came through the roof and landed right between them. That sure was close. There was a school nearby where we were, and an old lady was coming through the field next to it. A barrel landed right on top of her and killed her where she stood. They dropped stuff for two different days, and then a week later they dropped some more.

When I got back in Canada I was hospitalized for an operation on my kidney. My kidney was like a rotten apple and I was passing out quite often. It was because of that beating with the iron rod across my back. I needed surgery for other things as well.

We try and tell the young people about our experiences. We try and make them understand what we went through. They say that they don't believe it. We told them that we had to eat rats and grasshoppers and they didn't believe us. But it did happen, and I am proud of the service we gave for Canada.

My Grandparents

My Grampa Sid

Sarah Lucas, Age 10, Belle Anse Elementary School

I wish my Grampa Sid were alive to help me with this project. He was born and raised on Bonaventure Island and always had a good story to tell. He always talked about the days on the island before it became a national park. He told of the times crossing the ice from the island to the mainland in winter, with the ice cracking under the horses' feet, scared that the wagon would fall through. Often times the horse would stop, refusing to go any further because of a crack in the ice. My Grampa Sid would have to cover the crack with a blanket so the horse would move. In the summer, they would cross by boat.

Winters on the island were always cold and windy. There were many days that the people could not cross because of blowing snow and really big snowstorms. It was very scary for some because the doctor had to come from the mainland. With the help of his family, my Grampa Sid owned and ran the only hotel on the island, called the Bonaventure Lodge.

My great uncle would give tours with his horse and wagon all around the island, always stopping to see the thousands of gannets. I bet these tourists never imagined that one day this little island would become a national park. In 1973, my grampa and his family were forced to leave the island and bought a new hotel on the mainland. It is now called 'Auberge du Coin du Banc'. This is where the stories began. I remember seeing Grampa Sid rocking in the rocking chair by the old wood stove, pipe in mouth, starting every story with 'When we lived on the island...'

Life in the Good Old Days

As told by Flora Mullin

Flora was born in what used to be known as Brassett, now York, in 1936. She worked as a waitress at what used to be known as Mac's Restaurant, later known as Stanley's Restaurant. She still resides in Gaspé.

Flora Mullin and grandson Brian Fournier

My mother was such a handy woman; she could make something out of nothing at all. We watched her do just that most of our lives growing up. She was an incredible mother and was a real example to all eleven of us kids. She was a beautiful knitter, too. She didn't have any money to buy yarn, but the man next door would have his sheep sheared and he'd get her to knit him some underwear. He would give her some yarn for the underwear and she would make us mittens as well. She showed us how to make the best of any situation.

She would make our soap out of Gillet's lye and animal fat. She made us kids stay out of the back kitchen because she would be working with lye and it was poisonous. She used a big wooden tray to set the soap in once she had made it, then she cut the bars into 2-by-4 inch pieces of soap. We used the soap for about everything from shampooing our hair to washing dishes with the leftover shavings.

I remember running around with a picture of Robin Hood on my backside, more than once. My mother would wash the bags of flour and when she was finished with them, she would cut them into underwear for the girls.

Sometimes she didn't have any bleach so the colour stayed on the fabric for quite some time. Eventually it wore off after much wear. The only way to bleach clothes then was to wash them in hot water and put them out in the grass to dry.

We had no toothpaste when I was growing up. We used coals out of the stove to clean our teeth. My father used to take a few coals out when the fire was cooling down and he would set them aside on a pan or just leave them by the stove and let them cool. We would each take a coal and rub it all over our teeth. Our mouth would be covered in black, and then we had to brush it off with our fingers and a facecloth. We would wash our teeth every day with a facecloth and every second day with the coals. If you wanted white teeth, then this was the only way to do it. It tasted like wood, but it worked. We had the whitest teeth you can imagine, as white as snow.

If one of us had a toothache, my father would go and find a piece of a tree that had been hit by lightning. We would carry that piece of wood around with us in our pockets until the toothache was gone. Sometimes it would take an hour or two. I know that it works 'cause I used it for my own children. I used to get a lot of toothaches so I'd carry a piece of wood around with me in my pocket at all times as a precaution.

We used coarse salt to preserve our eggs. We would grease the eggs with pork fat, put them in the coarse salt and then cover them up. Every day we would go through the same routine of collecting the eggs and greasing 'em and putting 'em in the coarse salt. It felt really awful when you had to go and pick out the eggs later because they were all greasy and slimy, but the eggs kept all winter that way.

Now, buttermilk was great for sunburns, we never got blisters. Vinegar was used for everything in those days. If you'd scraped your knee, you'd put vinegar on it and use it for cleaning. We'd rinse our hair with vinegar and even today I sometimes rinse my hair with vinegar and water. It was good for everything.

We used to pick strawberries, blueberries, all kinds of berries. We were allowed to pick them but we weren't allowed to eat 'em, we had to bring the berries home for jam. We also picked chewing gum. I just loved picking chewing gum. It was so much fun when my father would take us back into the woods and teach us how to find the gum on the spruce trees in the spring and summer. There would be little lumps of chewing gum sticking out the side of the tree and we would pull it off and chew it just as fast as we could pick it. My brothers used to pick a lot of it and sell it for extra money.

Things sure are different now.

The Mullins

Brian Fournier, Age 11, Gaspé Elementary School

Once upon a time in the Gaspé, there was a family called the Mullins.

They made their own soap with fat from animals and made their own clothes.

They made their underwear from flour bags.

For toothpaste, they took coals from their stove and put some on their fingers and rubbed it on their teeth.

They washed their hair with homemade soap and rinsed it with vinegar. They washed their clothes on a washboard.

They used catalogue pages for bathroom tissue. For chewing gum, they chewed gum off of spruce trees.

When kids had a toothache their father looked for a piece of wood that was struck by lightning and the kid who had the toothache held the piece of wood and it would come better.

Their garden was 200 by 60 feet. When the kids came from school they watered the garden.

They kept a hen for their own eggs. On Sundays, father killed a hen for their Sunday dinner.

In the winter, they kept cows and pigs for milk and pork.

They would use coarse salt to preserve the eggs. They would put milk and cream in a brook to keep it cold. They would salt the beef and salt the pork if any was left in spring.

When a kid wanted to go outside he put on a pair of boots and his brothers and sisters would wait inside for him to return. When he came in, he gave the boots to the one next in line.

They used horse manure for a baseball or a hockey puck. They would play hopscotch, jump rope, tag and hide-and-seek as pastimes. They would use barrel staves for skis. If there was crusty snow, they would slide on cardboard.

For cleaning the snowy roads a horse would pass at 6 o'clock and make a path for everyone to walk on.

At dances, there would be only a man who played the fiddle for music.

Every person in the family knew how to play an instrument, father played mouth organ, mother played church organ and every child played the guitar or Jew's harp.

They had no ski-doo suits so they had long socks, knitted mittens and rubber boots.

Nobody knew how to skate. Only mother had skates, one year the oldest child would wear them, the next year the second oldest wore them, and so on.

For Christmas they would get an apple, a pair of mittens, skis made out of barrel staves, papers out of catalogues to make paper dolls.

Once a month father would go to the store in the Basin (Gaspé).

That was the life of people in 1940, '41, '42 and '43.

A Brush with Death

Brendan Rehel, Age 10, Belle Anse Elementary School
(Writing in Mansel Johnson's words)

Once upon a time, many years ago when I was a young man, chainsaws were not invented yet. Our source of heat was by wood so we had to use axes or a big wire saw called a bucksaw. So one day me and a friend of mine were walking home from a long day's work when a rain storm started. It was raining buckets when the lightning and thunder began. This wasn't our first time working in the rain, so no one was alarmed.

As we walked out of the woods, the axes on our shoulders and lunches in our hands, a sudden noise stopped me in my tracks. I seen a bright light and my body became very heavy as I fell to my knees. Minutes which seemed like hours slowly went by, when my friend Owen gently picked me up from the ground. To my surprise my axe was about fifteen feet from me. Owen tells me that when we were walking a lightning bolt came from the sky and hit directly on the sharp part of my axe. The jolt was so strong it blew the axe from my shoulder at least fifteen feet away. The only thing I can remember from my near brush with death is an awful headache and some sore muscles.

I am just grateful for the kind help from a good old friend.

How My Granny Lived 67 Years Ago

Janna Rutty, Age 9, Belle Anse Elementary School

One night in the Gaspé Coast, I went over to my granny's house. I asked her what was it like to live over 67 years ago. I even asked her how did they travel to school. How many miles did they walk? What happened during the years? And, what was Christmas like? She told me all kinds of stories. I found out they walked to school two miles with no ski-doo pants, just long stockings. They also had a lot of dances and parties. For Christmas, they had to make their own decorations. At night older people would get out their guitars. They sang, danced and played music.

My grandma had a lot of fun horseback riding. She used to feed the hens and the sheep and picked up the eggs. She liked to run the spinning wheel to twist the yarn made from the sheep's wool. Her mother would dye the yarn pretty colours and knit it into mittens, socks, scarves, sweaters and hats. Some of the wool for her clothes came from her favourite pet sheep, Jethro, whom she took very good care of when he was a baby.

I found out from listening to my granny that life back then was very different for a 10 year old girl. Her stories sounded interesting and exciting. I would like to live back 67 years ago so I wouldn't get bored so easily.

Grand Greve

Chad Langlois, Age 10, Gaspé Elementary School

Once upon a time in the Gaspé area there was a place called 'Grand Greve', that is where my grandmother came from. Her name is Irma Minchinton, this is a story she told me about life back then.

Granny was married to my grandfather, Alvin Langlois. For a living he worked on a boat called *The Labordock*. He was gone for months at a time, so Granny had to do all the work at home by herself. For example she looked after the home and the children. Granny and Grampa sure kept busy because they had fifteen children.

Granny said that the older children looked after the younger ones, while she made the bread and washed the clothes by hand.

Granny also said that fishing was a big thing in Grand Greve; a lot of families made their living on the water. When the fishermen saw the ring around the moon they said that bad weather was on the way and for them that wasn't a good thing: no fish, no profit.

Granny also told me that she liked to see Saturday night, because her and Grampa would get dressed up to go to the Grand Greve hall. There she would meet up with her friends and like Granny would say, 'Kick up her heels all night long!'

Also Granny said that she would go to the store and buy a chip and pop for 25 cents. That was really the good old days.

My Pappy

Colby Johnson, Age 6, Belle Anse Elementary School

This story is about my Pappy when he was a young boy growing up. When Pappy was about 7 years old he went to a small schoolhouse, not that far from his home, it was so close that he walked there everyday.

In grade 1 and 2 his teacher was Miss Jas Lipsey, she was a very nice person. Pappy used to daydream a lot in class, the things he was thinking on was about painting and who the

In Loving Memory of
Tennyson Johnson

artist was. The painters were Renoir and Jan Vermeer, etc.

Then in grade 3 and 4, he would look through magazines to see more paintings and to read more about the artist, also to find out where they came from.

At the age of 9 or 10, Pappy knew that he wanted to be a painter.

When in Miss Jas Lipsey's class he would draw pictures on the chalkboard, some of the things he drew were Santa Claus, reindeers, elves and also Santa's sleigh. Miss Lipsey liked his work so much that she bought some watercolours for Pappy and she encouraged Pappy to keep on painting.

Pappy used to go and hide away so he could work on his drawings. Other days Pappy would take his pocket-knife and start to whittle out little things, he made plaques and carvings, like a cowboy and horses, etc.

A few years later, Pappy started to make bigger things like snowshoes, skis and even moccasins to wear.

Still today my pappy paints and carves, now he makes fiddles and guitars, which are very beautiful, the sounds that come out of them are music to an angel's ears.

Pappy painted a picture of me, I was about 3 years old and it hangs on my wall with pride. I hope someday I could be like my pappy, having the skills to paint and carve.

Thanks Pap, for helping me with this story, it was lots of fun.

Mr. Herman Ste. Croix

Kelly Coombs, Age 8, Belle Anse Elementary School

Once upon a time on the Gaspé Coast, in a town called Barachois, a young man named Herman Ste. Croix was born on August 9th, 1919. Mr. Ste. Croix started to fish with his father and his Uncle Charlie in the middle of the boat at age 12.

In the 1930's, Mr. Ste. Croix's job was to bring in the fish, salted into stages in the tub after 3 to 4 days. Then he had to pull it up with horses to Coteau. The women used to take over, drying the fish on the flakes (made with flake wire and wood). Then the fish were taken down to Robin & Jones and graded out (the good from the bad).

Mr. Ste. Croix went on his own in logging when he was about 15 or 16 years old. Mr. Ste. Croix worked at the sawmill in Haldimand Town for about three years on night shift. He did 60 hours a week for $30 a month including room & board. There was no insurance, no compensation, no UI. The mill closed down. Then he went into the Army from 1940 to 1941, but was discharged because of his back.

Then he met his wife-to-be (Eva Element) and married in November 1945. They had three children. They raised them on the 2e Rang Nord (Coteau) on the land. He was 26 years old. They lived on fishing, logging and mining (1953 – Murdochville Copper Mine; 1957 – Elliot Lake, Ontario). He was working at the Camp International and came home with lots of lice. His wife was taking care of the kids and house. He saw her start knitting mittens and socks by the oil lamp and have them ready for morning. There was no power, no radio and the first paper came out in 1948 called *The Family Herald*.

Those Annett Men

Matthew Annett, Age 11, Gaspé Elementary School

Not just whaling and fishing: Those Annett Men with a moose

Once upon a time my grandfather, Victor William Annett, the seventh son of Charles William Annett, the grandson of William Annett, told me a story.

His grandfather William lived in the time of whaling in the Gaspé Bay, in the Gulf of St. Lawrence. Whaling was a tradition handed down from one generation to the next. His great-grandfather came from England with his wife Elizabeth Siddon in 1770. He was the first Annett whaler in Gaspé. In order to go whaling, one had to build a boat and make the equipment.

When a whale was spotted, the fishermen would get as close as possible and throw a harpoon by hand into the whale. The harpoon was made of iron with a barb on the end of it like a fishhook. This would prevent the harpoon from pulling out. The whale would try to escape, sometimes pulling the boat for many miles. When the whale would get tired they would haul the whale to the shore.

Once the whale was onshore the fishermen would cut blubber off the whale and 'try it out' or boil it in a large pot made like a soup bowl. This pot was about five feet across and about two and a half feet deep. There is still one of those pots at the old homestead. A considerable amount of oil was obtained by this method. The whale oil was very useful in the Gaspé area. For instance, the lighthouse in Cap des Rosiers in 1858 operated on whale oil for twenty years. A 30-gallon barrel of oil was worth about $30. The young humpback whale was considered as good as beef to eat. The skin could also be converted into leather.

Those Annett men were known to be tall and broad-shouldered. That would have been a considerable advantage. The first Annett who came to Gaspé was known as Captain Annett and was said to have been six feet, five inches tall and considered a giant in his time. The traditional whaling finished in the 1890's.

Now with the whaling finished, William took up salmon net fishing in York Bay. In order to be able to fish he needed a smaller boat and a net. He had to knit the net by hand. He also had to have a boathouse. This was a small building in which they could eat and sleep in while tending the nets. This boathouse could also float up or down the bay with the tide. The salmon fishing with nets finished in the Upper York Bay in 1927.

In the summer months, William was kept busy with farming, along with whaling and fishing. In the winter months he cut firewood, which had to be chopped by axe into stove lengths. In 1908 he bought a saw machine, which was operated by horse thread. This would prove to be much easier than the chopping had been. In 1911, he bought a gasoline three h.p. motor, which weighed nine hundred pounds. It had lots of power to run the saw machine and the thrasher machine. The thrasher was used to separate the oats from the straw.

In winter months he also did trapping up the York River to where Murdochville is today. To be able to trap, he needed snowshoes that were made by hand. He also took a dog or two with a sleigh. He was very concerned about the weight of his load. He even considered the size and weight of the rope used to tie on his load. His sleigh was made with the lightest wood, being cedar. He would also take a tent and fold-down stove with telescopic pipes.

He also had small camps that he called fireside camps in which there was no stove. They made the camp with one straight wall and a leaning wall. There was an opening on the top for the smoke to go out. It would take about nine days to set traps and go about sixty miles, where Murdochville is today. Once they had arrived at their destination, they would stay and trap the area for about two weeks.

The upper part of the York River had only a jumper trail which is just big enough for a horse and sleigh to pass. Sometimes there was no trail at all. His trip would take about a month.

My grandfather told this story about his grandfather on Sunday, November 14, 2004.

Like a Hub to a Wheel

Chelsea Flowers, Age 16, Gaspé Polyvalent School

Gaspé is truly unique, not only by its landscape, but also because of the people. Over time, Gaspé has certainly evolved into a bustling mini-city. However, back in the earlier 1920's, Gaspé certainly was dissimilar from modern day. My grand-mother, Alma Adams, who was born in the 1920's, distinctly remembers her childhood. She claims, in these times, life revolved around family and farming but most of all religion.

Once upon a time in Gaspé, religion was the center of everything. Religion to the town was like a hub to a wheel. Mrs. Adams recalls three distinct occasions in her childhood in which religion impacted her greatly.

It was the time of the Spanish Flu, better known as influenza, and every second person seemed to be ill. The entire town of St. Majorique, Gaspé seemed to be infected and graves were being dug daily. Much to my grandmother's mother's horror, her husband fell ill to influenza. My great-grandmother was convinced he would perish, but was also convinced the family could not survive without him. Desperate, she prayed to the Lord when her husband fell into a coma and asked him to spare her husband, but instead take three of her children. Without him, she knew none of her children would survive. Miraculously, a week later my great-grandfather awoke, but only to find three of his children dead. This amazingly did happen and only strengthened my great-grandmother's faith in God.

Another incident occurred during a horrific fire. A great forest fire struck the whole town in the 1920's, it spread widely and quickly, destroying many homes and lives. My great-grandmother, desperate to save her house from the fast approaching fire, decided to put her faith in the Lord. In the barn, which was closest to the blaze, she tacked up a paper picture of Mother Mary. Again, she prayed to the Lord to not let the fire take their home and to let the picture of the Virgin Mary protect them. Supernaturally, the fire stopped at the barn. However, before the fire ceased, the entire barn did burn ... all except the picture of Mother Mary. People from miles around came to the miracle of the Mother Mary picture, in which only the border was burned, not the circular photo.

Another example of religion in the 1920's is the 'Great Flood'. For a week straight, a heavy rain loomed over the Gaspé. The water began to rise and soon overtook the river and flooded the land. Finally, the water came so high that my great-grandmother feared they would have to leave their house. Yet again, my grandmother's mother had faith. Though dangerous, she proceeded out into the storm and placed a religious article on a tree stump close to the house. To my grandmother and the rest of the children, she stated they would only leave if the water were to pass the stump. So they prayed together, hoping for a miracle. Fortunately, they did get their miracle. The water rose to within an inch of the stump. Again, their faith in the Lord had saved them.

These miraculous events really did occur. Because of these events, my grandmother still has great faith in the Lord. She feels that religion not only had a great impact on her family in the 'old days' but all of Gaspé as well.

THE MI'KMAQ

Gesgapegiag and Wagatasg

As told by Bernard Jerome

Born in 1947 in Gesgapegiag, Bernard has always been keenly interested in the culture and history of his people. He currently works for the Mi'gmawei Mawiomi Secretariat, mapping the traditional use of resources. Bernard's pastimes include making hand drums, wood and soapstone carving, and occasionally lacing snow-shoes.

Mine was a traditional family. I was one of fourteen children in a house where only our native tongue was spoken. The first seven years of my life were totally in Mi'kmaq.

Starting school at the age of 7 was very difficult. It was like an alien culture to me. I had known nothing but the Mi'kmaq culture and language up to that point. School was my introduction into other worlds, worlds I didn't know

Bernard Jerome

existed. I had a difficult time learning the English language as I didn't understand a word they were saying. It was quite a learning experience.

I didn't know what TV was until I was 14. We had a radio but our main source of entertainment was the stories the elders were always telling. There's one story in particular I remember; the story about the Pug La de moog or the 'little' people. The Pug La de moog used to live on Mount Carleton and if you wandered off into the woods too far, they'd kidnap you and drag you away, keeping you overnight and then releasing you in the morning. The elders told that story to make sure the young ones didn't wander off and we didn't. We didn't even try. Such stories go back many generations and have become a tradition.

My uncle, George Caplin, was very well known for his stories and teachings, as well as for the snowshoes and moccasins he made. He had his own way of teaching. Instead of moulding you, he'd model you. When he taught, he shared his experiences with you; survival skills, even tanning hides. I used to watch him do it and when I shot my very first otter, Uncle George showed me how to tan the hide. It was my father, however, who showed me how to skin a bear at the young age of 13 – an unpleasant experience and one I've not relived.

I remember playing the Waltes game when I was young. It's a dice game, and it has six dice made of moose antlers, and a bowl made of maple with sticks as counters. This game would help kids count at an early age. It's a Mi'kmaq game, a game of chance, as it deals with numbers and possibilities. We also used the Waltes for fortune telling, and now it's making a comeback.

Yes, my childhood was a traditional one filled with traditional beliefs. I cannot say it was a difficult life. I cannot say that we were ever poor. We were provided with the needs of life and I believe I had a very rich life. This history of the Gesgapegiag Mi'kmaq is very rich as well, here is a well-known story that has been passed down by the elders...

Many, many years ago there lived a group of Mi'kmaq along the shores of the Bay of Chaleur, in the region of the seventh district of the Mi'kmaq Nation.

The Mi'kmaq were known as Gesgapegiawag, or the wandering people, after years of nomadic life in search of land as foretold by the elders. They finally came upon this land of which a child had dreamt of and established a community on the estuary of the Gesgapegiag River, where the river widens and turns to salt. Their leader, Wagatasg, chose this area for its richness and beauty. It is a place which the Spirit has set aside for its children.

To the East, the land of the eagle and the rising sun, there are the medicines of sweet grass, muskrat root, tobacco and teas from various plants. There is also shellfish, whale, seal and other species.

To the South, the land of the turtle and mid-day, there is the warm salty bay, which Mi'kmaq have used for preserving foods for the winter months. More often salt from the bay was used as an antibiotic medicine. It is the direction from where the salmon, bass, eel and other water species come. Other species during the late part of summer can be seen such as the otter, geese, mallards and the turtle.

To the West, the land of thunder and of the setting sun, there is much to be had. The swampland provides us with plants of medicine, food and shelter. The medicine of the wetland consists of sweet-grass, cranberry, alder and other species. The food that the West provides is potatoes, corn, wheat and other grains, deer, elk and porcupine which were used for food, clothing and crafts. Cedar, spruce, juniper and poplar were also abundant.

To the North, land of the Bear: caribou, beaver, moose and other fur-bearing animals were also available to the Mi'kmaq.

The Gesgapegiag River was the main provider of the region for transportation in hunting, fishing and harvesting, for this is the place where maple trees provided maple sugar in the spring of the year, the black ash provided for baskets and snowshoe frames, birch provided bark for canoes, dwellings and household items such as cookware. The toboggan was also made of birch wood strips. Along the shores of the Gesgapegiag River the Mi'kmaq harvested foods such as fiddleheads, mint, hazelnuts and bush cranberries.

Considering the northerly location, the climate is exceptionally mild during the year. The warm breeze of the bay to the south and the mountain range to the north influence the weather.

Wagatasg was a brave and wise Mi'kmaq leader of Gesgapegiag. Long before he was born, it had been prophesied by the elders that the day would come when a child would be born amongst the Mi'kmaq to teach and lead them. It was said that there would be a sign on the day of the child's birth: Mother Earth would close her eyes at noon and darkness would come over her, for a brief period, as if night-time.

One mid-summer day of the seventh month, the wisdom of the elders was revealed. First, at mid-day, came a heavy silence, as if all life had lost its voice. When the Mi'kmaq looked up to the sky, they could see Grandmother Moon move toward the front of Grandfather Sun and cast her shadow over Mother Earth.

Witnessing the event, the elders of the community summoned the warriors and ordered them to build a sacred fire fitting for The Great Spirit. The elders of great vision offered medicines to the fire. Once the offering was complete, the elders told the Mi'kmaq that the day had come. Today, in the seventh wigwam they would witness the prophecy come true.

High upon the tall pine tree, as if in harmony, the raven spoke and a great eagle circling high above added his voice. At this time the Mi'kmaq heard the wail of a newborn child. As soon as it had begun, Grandmother Moon moved off to the west, allowing Grandfather Sun to again bless Mother Earth with his golden light. The Mi'kmaq rejoiced and feasted for seven days. Truly, the event that the elders had spoken of so long ago had come, just as they had predicted.

The seasons came and went and Wagatasg and the Mi'kmaq of Gesgapegiag enjoyed the bounty that Mother Earth provided for them. So it went for seven times eleven years and the Mi'kmaq knew that soon their brave warrior, Wagatasg, would leave on a great journey.

After the harvest, the Mi'kmaq prepared for the coming harsh winter months. Wagatasg would sit by the fire and share stories, songs, laughter and joy. One evening, as they sat around the fire, the people sensed that something was not right with Wagatasg, he was quiet and his mind was drawn to the sky. Wagatasg stood up and summoned his people to the fire. Wagatasg had mixed feelings of the message he had for the Mi'kmaq. With his soft trembling voice he informed his beloved people that his time had come, according to prophecy, to go on to the great journey of the spirit world. The Mi'kmaq remembered what the elders had told years ago: they must prepare for the long journey. It was told that on the seventh day of the eleventh month, their leader and the Mi'kmaq must travel north to the mountain and wait for a sign, as someone calling from the Skite'kmuju-awti (Spirits' Road or Milky Way). As they approached the summit, they saw a great glare of light high in the sky. It flickered and danced, and radiated toward them. The Mi'kmaq gathered close and made a circle around Wagatasg to help for the journey.

Suddenly, a flash of light sliced through the night sky, blinding everyone around Wagatasg. When their eyes recovered from the blinding flash, they realized that Wagatasg was no longer among them. He had gone to join the spirit of the night sky and is among the spirits we now know as the Wagatasg (Northern Lights).

Today, north of Gesgapegiag, there is a mountain known as Besge'ameneg, meaning, 'a cut off' or 'a short way'. If you were to look out your window toward the North, on the seventh day of the eleventh month, you will witness the dance of Wagatasg, the spirits of the sky, for Wagatasg is still watching over his people.

The Legend of the Invisible Man

Corey Thomas & John Gedeon Jr., Age 13, Wejgwapniag School

The invisible man was a person who could turn invisible. He was looking for a girl to marry. He would turn invisible and hunt for a girl to marry but when he would appear the girls would run away. There was this one girl who was always pushed around by her sisters and mother. She was made to do chores that were not hers to do.

So one day, the invisible man was hunting and had caught a bear. He was carrying the bear across a big field that was next to the river. He then stumbled across this girl who had been mistreated by her sisters and mother. When he appeared she was not frightened.

The girl spoke to the invisible man but her family did not know whom she was talking to. The sister said in a mean voice, 'Keep doing your chores.' The invisible man appeared and the sisters and mother ran to the elders. The elders were in the distance in a wigwam.

The elders arrived and said, 'What is wrong with you? Whom are you talking to?' The girl replied, 'My friend, he has come from a distant land'.

The four elders said, 'Let's sit down and talk.' The elders could not see the invisible man saying, 'This man you speak of, is he good for you? Are you going to leave with him?'

The girl replied, 'Maybe.'

The elders asked, 'Is he here in this wigwam with us now?'

The girl replied, 'Yes, you cannot see him?' She was pointing towards thin air to the naked eye. Then the elders heard, 'Why are you talking about me?'

The elders asked, 'Who is this?' and the voice replied, 'It is me, the true love of your granddaughter.'

The elders said, 'If you take my granddaughter with you, you shall respect her or my men shall find you.' And then the invisible man replied, 'Agreed.'

So, the invisible man married the girl. They made two children. One name Gitpu (Eagle) and the other child name Wogwis (Fox).

The Mi'kmaq People

Draven Bernard Jerome, Age 9, Wejgwapniag School

I chose to write my story about my own people, the Mi'kmaq. I believe that it is really important to share our interest and our values, and that they are strong and alive.

Many years ago, we used to have a strong communication line. My dad tells me that our people use to have gatherings that we call Pow-wows. They would dance and eat and share stories with each other. At one time, when my dad was a kid he used to go to school to learn to become an Indian dancer. Our elders taught him.

They used to go to other schools and show the other people what they had learned. Then one time this movie company came to our reserve to ask if they could do movies about us. The movies were called *Indian Legends*. Today sometimes they still show these movies. The TV people wanted to learn the ways of the Indian about hunting, fishing and survival.

My home is called Gesgapegiag, which means where the river widens. In our community we fish and hunt. In the month of June, we fish salmon and we hunt moose and deer in the fall. It is a tradition when a hunter kills a moose or deer, he or she first feeds his family. Then, if he or she kills another, it is tradition to share with the community.

FISHING

A Fisherman's Day in 1910

David Langlois, Age 15, Gaspé Polyvalent School

My father told me about his grandfather, Nelson Langlois. Born in 1896, he started fishing when he was 10 years old. He got up at 2:30 am with a coal oil lantern and walked down the landing (down a 60-foot cliff) in Cape Gaspé. On the beach he pushed the dory from the high watermark to the water and went to haul his herring nets before going to his 30-foot fishing boat. Then he would sail out about 1,000 feet offshore and use a hand line or long line to get groundfish.

When the early evening breeze would come that's when he would go in. When he got back to shore he used a pew (a pitchfork type stick) to throw the fish on land. In the dark with his coal oil lantern, he would split the fish on his table on the beach and throw it in the barrel he had full of water beside the table leg. Then he would put the fish into a hand barrel and lift it up the cliff with a boom. He would pull his dory back to place then he put the fish in salt barrels in the shed nearby.

After a long day of work he finished at around 6 pm and would go have his supper.

The Big Fish

Erin McWhirter, Age 16, Bonaventure Polyvalent School

Colin Gedeon, Esmond B. Martin and Lonnie Willett with 55½ pounder

One day on the Gaspé in 1939 a man by the name of Esmond B. Martin caught the largest Atlantic salmon ever taken in North American waters, here on our own river the Grand Cascapedia. Although we take it for granted, this river is considered one of the ten best salmon fishing rivers in the world.

Esmond Martin was only a young man in his twenties when he came to the river in June of 1939. He was here visiting his Aunt Amy Guest, who at the time owned her own private fishing camp called New Derreen. Young Martin loved fly-fishing for Atlantic salmon, but he was a novice. Like so many other first-timers, Esmond failed to catch anything except a few trout in his first two weeks of fishing. The river was teeming with trout and he caught his share of them, but it was a salmon that he was trying to land. His Aunt Amy was an expert angler and spent most of her summer fishing the waters of the Cascapedia. Before young Esmond arrived she had spotted a large fish. It had first showed itself in Home Pool a couple of days before. Every guide on the river and just about everybody else, including his Aunt Amy, knew there was a giant fish somewhere in the river.

Esmond and his guides, Colin Gedeon and Lonnie Willett, had been fishing Maple Pool, a favourite one just above Home Pool. As they were covering the water halfway through, the guide thought he had seen some movement, so they decided to fish through the pool again. Everyone had the big fish on their minds. Everyone wanted to be the lucky angler to brag about it. At about the middle of the second pass through the pool, history took the fly. The fish never had a chance.

The record fish of 55½ pounds was caught on a Lady Amherst fly. The Lady Amherst was better known at the time as 'Cascapedia's favourite fly'. George Bonbright, a fisherman from the United States, created the famous fly while fishing on the Cascapedia in the early 1920's. The trophy fish's measurements were 49¾ inches long, also 30⅛ inches in girth.

When Esmond went back to New Derreen Camp to proudly show off his prize catch, his Aunt Amy was not impressed. In fact she was very angry with him and felt that he should have left the fish in the river for her to catch. After he left the Cascapedia that year, his aunt did not invite him back.

After word got out, everybody wanted to see the famous fish. At every station on the return trip to New York, the fish had to be hauled out and exhibited to an admiring public. By the time the fish made it back to New York, Esmond had made arrangements to have the fish professionally stuffed and mounted by a taxidermist.

For a period of time this fish was in the American Museum of Natural History. Today the family of the late Mr. Martin still have the prize fish mounted proudly in their home.

The Martin fish became part of the fishing folklore of the Cascapedia. In the record books there have been approximately seventeen giants of 50 pounds and over taken from its waters. Today fishermen still come to this world famous river hoping to catch the 'big one'.

Kingfishers for a Quarter

As told by Richard Hunt

Kingfishers used to catch all the little salmon and that's not good for salmon fishing. The Gaspésia Company would pay anyone who could get rid of them. I used to get 25 cents a bill for kingfishers.

I would put a post out by the river with a trap on it. The kingfishers would land on the post and get caught in the trap when they tried to go after the salmon. I would get four or five a day.

I used to put all the bills in a bottle of salt water – a big jar. I'd take it down to Gaspésia and get my pay. The poor kingfishers though, you had to kill them, you couldn't just cut their beak off. I felt bad doing it. Now there aren't many kingfishers left; I must have caught them all!

Just Like Brothers

As told by Dudley Le Maistre

Dudley was born in Sayabec in 1925 and resided equally throughout his life in Beaconsfield and on the Gaspé Coast. He worked at Robin's in his 20's and then taught French in Montreal. He loved cooking, gardening and his summers in the Gaspé. Dudley passed away in 2002.

Along the Coast, sports fishing for salmon was just amazing. People were very keen on it. Some of the camps were like mini-palaces, because the men that came here to fish were very well-to-do. They were so busy back in the cities, and they might have been very wealthy, but they wanted to get away from all that. It was mostly Americans, by far, that came to fish. The fishermen and the guides – they were all very close on all of these rivers.

I once knew an old man who worked on the Restigouche as a guide. One of the men he guided, an American man, was enormously wealthy. He died, and I remember reading his obituary in *Time* magazine. He left an enormous fortune behind. And he left something like 30,000 or 40,000 to this old guide. The two of them got along like brothers and the wealth wasn't important to either one of them. It's quite a wonderful story you know, because he was just about to retire and he wasn't a wealthy man. Everybody in the area knew just what that meant to him at his old age.

Poachers

As told by Winston Tozer

Winston was born in Cullens Brook in 1940 and was a warden on the Bonaventure for 34 years. He now runs a saw mill that has been in his family for years and resides in Fauvel.

When I was a game warden we had a few poachers every year. I'm sure they still do it today. We did a lot of night canoeing when I worked on the river. There are 30 miles of river and we'd do about twelve to fifteen miles a night, if we thought there was poaching going on.

When we caught someone we'd get all of their nets. We had lots of fun and rough times while we were doing it. We'd seize everything that was there. Sometimes they'd take off into the woods – we couldn't do much about that, but we'd pick up their equipment. We were never armed, but the poachers sometimes were. I've been shot at, but they were never good shots.

ADVENTURES

Little Boy on a Leash

By Gerard Poirier

Trouble's brewing! Jimmy Gillis and Ricky Mullin

René Lévesque's mother, like all moms, worried about her little boy. In the case of this little boy in particular, her concern was fully justified. There was no way in this world of knowing what this little guy was going to do next, or where he was going to turn up. He could be standing there right by you one moment, and then, before your very eyes, he would do a disappearing act. Some kids have that faculty. They can seemingly vanish into thin air, leaving you to wonder what in the name of heaven happened to them, while wishing you could do the same thing.

René's parents had something to worry about there. They feared that the boy's impromptu wanderings might get him into trouble. They wracked their brains looking for a solution to this very real problem, and finally came up with one. They got a long length of good strong rope, fastened one end around his waist and the other end to the post of the veranda. The rope, of course, was knotted behind René's back where his busy little fingers couldn't reach, and at the same time, it was long enough to allow him to roam over most of the yard, but not to get out of it.

Now, under that restriction, René obviously could not come and play in our yard. No problem. We simply moved our base of operations over to his yard. He had the toys; we had the gang.

Everything went just fine for a good while. His parents came and checked regularly, and were pleased to see that we were all having a good time within the bounds set by René's leash. Even the boy himself seemed to accept this severe restriction on his movements; as long as we were all with him inside this little open-air prison, that is. When the time arrived for us to move a little further afield, as was sure to happen sooner or later, it might be just another story altogether. We would have to wait and see.

Soon, winter was upon us with its thick coat of snow. Away went scooters and bicycles and all the other summer toys. Out came toboggans, sleds, and, of course, heavy winter clothes. René was still rope-restricted.

A heavy snowstorm with strong winds had made a very high snowdrift near the Lévesque house. A beautiful place to slide. René suggested that we try it with the toboggan, and he himself made the seating arrangements. I was to sit in the front, he would sit in the middle and Paul would take the rear position. I remember suggesting that it might be better if René sat in the back, but he insisted on the other position.

O.K. let's go! Down the hill we went, picking up speed all the way. And everything went just fine ...until we reached the end of the rope.

Well, the post of the veranda held firm, and so did the rope, but René was pulled back with a bone-jarring yank, taking with him poor Paul whose face smashed into the back of the little fellow's head, which thankfully was covered with an extra-heavy cloth cap, allowing Paul to hang on to his teeth, although I'm sure they were all badly loosened. As for me, sitting in the front of the toboggan, I had a lovely problem-free ride. So much so in fact, that I suggested another one. I was voted down, however. First, by a fellow whose head was still spinning, and then, by another one who had almost been cut in two. We'd have to find another way...

At any rate, Paul and I had to leave. We had to go to church, this was Sunday and there was no way out of it.

Because it was winter, these prayer sessions known as Vespers were held in the afternoon rather than the evening. Mom had reminded us of this during lunch hour, knowing that we had a tendency to be forgetful of certain things; like going to church, for instance.

So, we said so long to our friend René. We'd see him after church we told him. He looked at us as we walked away and we knew that this would be the supreme test. Would the rope hold him? It was a strong one; but then, that boy had more tricks in his bag than a magician.

Twenty minutes later, Paul and I were in church praying as hard as we could and being very attentive to what was going on. Vespers were sung by the regular church choir, and I remember how I used to enjoy the singing. They took place at a more civilized hour too, instead of before daylight like early morning mass. Getting up while it was still dark, in the cold of winter, was almost a shock to my system.

Well, the melodious, peaceful atmosphere of the church was not to last. What we had feared at the time of our last look at René had happened. The boy was loose, and was now making his entrance into the house of prayer. There he was, walking straight down the centre aisle, dressed in his heavy winter clothes, and trailing about six feet of rope behind him, one end of which was still securely fastened to his waist. He looked in all directions as he advanced to the front of the church, and Paul and I knew very well he was looking for us. We put our heads down and our hands in front of our faces, as though in deep meditation. We didn't want anybody to think that we knew this little guy. René, however, had no such compunctions. He didn't care about anything except finding us, and he soon did. He came over, jumping across the pews until he got to us. And then, in a voice that could easily be heard all over the church, he said: 'Hey, what are you fellows doing here? C'mon, we'll go slide some more!'

When we saw that he wouldn't be ignored, we tried to keep him quiet, but that only made matters worse, and soon we were making as much noise as he was. The music and the singing had stopped, the priest was giving us a petrifying look, and all heads were turned in our direction.

Paul and I didn't know what to do, except maybe choke the little son-of-a-gun. That might have worked outdoors, but we knew we'd never get away with it in church.

A man sitting in a nearby pew came to our aid. His invaluable help was in the form of a suggestion. Quite simple really, but we were too mad at the little service-disturber to even think properly.

The man said to us, 'Why don't you both go out with him? That would be better than staying in here and wrecking Vespers.' He might have added that the priest was probably getting set to kick us all out too. Paul and I walked out, with René following us like a little pup.

I could not be sure of this, but I thought I heard a big sigh of relief as we went out the door. Perhaps it was just my imagination, and then again, maybe not.

The Incredible Bottomless Hole

Léandra Desjardins, Age 15, Bonaventure Polyvalent School

Steven Dow of Port Daniel smiles as I request from him a story or legend of the Gaspé Coast.

'Does it have to be a true one?' he asks.

'Not necessarily entirely true,' I reply.

'Well this is a true one,' affirms Steven.

Not so long ago, on the top of the Port Daniel Mountain, which at the time was owned by a certain Mr. Alan Mahan there was, and still is, an incredible bottomless hole.

Now it was rumoured that one could drop a pebble in the pit and never hear it hit the bottom, which however was only townsfolk superstition. Until one morning Alan Mahan brought his cows that had been grazing on the mountain home to milk. After counting and recounting he realized that one was missing and so he went back to the mountain in search of it. He soon found tracks that led straight to… the pit! Now Alan was a brave man but the sound of the desperate mooing of the frightened animal and its great body hitting the sides of the pit as it made its endless journey downwards into the abyss of darkness nearly frightened the bejesus out of him.

At first the people doubted Alan's seemingly crazy story until they, too, stood near the pit (but not too close) and heard the slightly fainter moaning of the helpless cow, and that was a week later!

Nobody dared to approach the pit for a long-time until at length it lost all its reality and became a simple story. Yet even today, Steven tells me earnestly that if I should ever come across a hole on the top of Port Daniel Mountain I should listen carefully and maybe, just maybe, I might hear something.

The Legend of the Burning Ship
Danielle Jerome, Age 11, Wejgwapniag School

YOU may have seen a boat, YOU may have seen a whale but did YOU ever see a burning ship in the bay? HERE IS WHAT MY GRANDFATHER TOLD ME:

When my grandfather was a fisherman in Hopetown on the Chaleur Bay, his partner and he were fishing. They heard screams and they looked out onto the bay. But, they could not see anyone on board the ship. As they got closer, the ship would get further and further away.

Once my grandfather and partner realized they could not get close to the ship, they went back to shore. They realized that it was not a real ship, they looked back to see the ship again and it had vanished. It was the legendary 'Burning Ship.' My grandfather was really scared but now he believed in the supernatural.

TRANSPORTATION

Working the Rails

As told by Roland Prentice

Roland was born in New Brunswick on December 25, 1924. He moved to New Carlisle in 1940 and started to work for the CNR in 1948. He still resides in New Carlisle.

I used to spend my summers as the resident railroad water boy. I started when I was 14 years old. I'd carry the water for the men to drink in them days. You may have seen the old buckets that you carried over your shoulder. We used to go along with the men working and if they wanted a drink of water, then they would take the ladle and have a little drink. We used to get big money in those days; I think we got ten cents an hour.

Oh, the CNR was a great place to work. All of us fellows got along; we had lots of laughs together. I came back after the war and started working for the CNR again as a fireman, but not a fireman in the typical sense. Back then, firemen would shovel coal into the steam engines. That lasted until 1952 when they brought in the diesel trains.

I eventually became an engineer. Did you know that each trestle has a different sound? You get to know where you are on the tracks. You can actually recognize the sounds of each of the crossings. It's the same with steam engines. We would get to know the sound of the engines, each one is fired differently. An old fella once told me, he said, 'Let me tell you, young fellow, if you're going to fire a steam engine, let me tell you something. They're like women and no woman is the same, they're all different. Get to know her by her number, because she's like that.' And he was right, I came to learn that each steam engine fired differently, each engine was unique. After a while you could tell how many shovels of coal it would take to go up a hill, depending on which number engine we had.

I killed a nice-looking moose one morning passing through Black Cape. I didn't mean to, I said to the other engineer, 'I'm not going to kill this moose' and I slowed right down to allow him time to pass over the tracks. He was stepping off the track, but then his hoof got caught on one of the ties and he fell down. The train passed over his neck and broke it. We stopped and dug a hole to bury the moose.

Moose weren't the only things on the tracks besides the train. Some days cars would try to race us at the crossings. They were fearless, tempting fate and trying to get across the tracks before the train had crossed. I would call the brakeman and say, 'Missed him this time. The next time he'll be even bolder and when that train hits him, he'll be lucky to get out of it alive.'

Holy Jumpin'! The year of Expo in Montreal, I think it was 1967, every driver went foolish. Sid Scott was braking with me one time and he told me that he was just a nervous wreck. I said, 'Not me, they can't reach me up here.' There were a terrible pile of them risking their lives; they'd beat us to the crossing, and half a mile down the track, they'd be sitting on their gallery watching us go by. They were always in such a hurry. Hundreds of 'em.

There were a lot of people walking along the tracks, too. Once when I was driving the train I saw a girl walking along the track. I tooted the horn and rang the bells but she didn't move off the track. I put the train on emergency stop right away. And when you do that, everything on the train shuts down. But this time the train had seventy cars on it and the weight of those seventy cars kept pushing it forward. I even put the engine brakes on, which we weren't supposed to use, but I couldn't kill that girl so I put them on. With no more than five feet between us and her, she suddenly turned around and saw the train, must have felt the vibrations or something. She jumped to the side and we rolled on by. The brakeman got out to see what had happened and when he got back on the train, he said she didn't hear us coming because she had her Walkman on. That's a dangerous thing to do, you know.

Another time my brother George was conducting with me in the engine. Now, west of the station in Chandler there's a bridge that crosses the river. That day there were four girls on the bridge with their bikes. When we came around the turn and saw them, I put the train on emergency stop right away, and I said to George, 'I'm killing them all, there's no way I'm going to be able to stop.' I cut the engine, because without that the wheels can't move. And we came to a full stop just before the bridge. One of the girls had fallen and had her leg stuck between the ties. They were only four inches apart and she was stuck there. George and I got out and went to help and hauled her out without breaking her leg. By then the people from the cottages nearby were running up to the train. They saw it stopped and they thought the girls were all dead. Well, they were just so glad that the kids were alive. You know, you can't run on a trestle when there is a train coming, because of the gaps in the ties. It's real easy to trip.

Another time we were going up to Matapedia and we had the plough on and were passing by the crossing in Black Cape. When we came to the crossing, the wing of the plough would dump snow, slush and salt. All I could see was the windshield of a car and the snow going straight for it. I thought, 'Those people are going to be dead ducks because everything just got dumped on them.' We managed to get to the car, which was stopped about eight feet from the crossing, and there were two women in it. Those poor women! We opened the door and they were in some kind of a mess. The car was full of snow and slush. It was even in the backseat. One woman said, 'I heard the whistle blowing and I heard the bell in the engine, but why didn't you fellows stop?'

'Madam,' I said, 'let me tell you something. You are supposed to stop at least fifty feet from the crossing because that is CNR property and you have to be that distance away. If you come up to eight feet from the crossing, you're going to get dumped on because the plough will clean itself at the crossing.' Then a policeman showed up and he asked what had happened. She said, 'They broke my windshield.' The policeman looked at me and said, 'Jeez, look at the mess of their car.' I said, 'She's lucky she's alive. Had she come a little closer it might have killed her you know.' That plough was moving at twenty miles an hour and it was up so high it smashed her windshield.

Those are just the near misses I remember. We had a lot of good times on the train, too. One time there was a bunch of us heading to Gaspé and Elmer Astels was with us. We were all in the van and we were sitting on those long benches. Arnold came in the van and he said, 'Elmer, look what I found!' He was holding a little mouse. Well, Elmer hopped up and he jumped right out of the van! The train was moving at a good speed, too. You know it's a good job we weren't going over a trestle or something, because he would have been killed. Mitchell grabbed the cord and we put the train on emergency stop to get Elmer. When we got Elmer back he said, 'Holy jumpin' Willy, am I ever terrified of them mice, eh!?'

We had lots of good laughs in those days, working for the CNR. Not many of us are left now to tell the old stories. We had a lot of good, clean fun.

The Train

As told by Rowena Cunning

Rowena was born in Sandy Beach in 1913 into a family of eight children. Before she was married and had her own family of five, she earned 50 cents a day housekeeping. Rowena loved working outdoors on their small farm and she loved to dance. Today, she enjoys reading and spending her winters in Pierrefonds with her daughter.

When the trains first came in to Gaspé, I didn't travel on them a lot. My first trip on the train was 67 years ago. Elsie Pye and I went to Douglastown for the day. We made so many plans about that trip – you'd have thought we were going to England, I tell you! It was an exciting event. The next time I travelled on the train was 64 years ago. I went to Corner-of-the-Beach for a Women's Institute picnic.

The first trip I made to Montreal by train was about 55 years ago, and I've made a good many trips since. Those were the old coal trains. There weren't many people travelling back then, so they only had one passenger car. I remember when they used to pull into the station. We could hear them blowing the horn down here, and we'd run to the track to see if we could make it before the train arrived. It didn't move too fast back then.

We Have Arrived!

As told by Lionel Gilker

Lionel was born in 1916 in New Carlisle and joined the Canadian National Railways in 1941, a position he held until his retirement in 1977, with the exception of the war years in which he served in the Canadian Air Force. He enjoyed hunting and fishing and was an active member of the community. Fondly known as 'Paddy', Lionel passed away in 2002.

I started working on the railroad in January of '41, and I worked there for 36 years, taking out time for the service. I was in the Air Force for almost five years. I was on the ground crew, service police. We would secure the station and I did a lot of traveling too, it was a requirement that there be a security person on the train.

I worked on both the passenger and the freight train, but mostly on the freight. I was a doctor in training when they first started. There was more money to be made on the freight train, but it meant longer hours, sometimes eighteen-hour days. The freight trains used to haul anything that was coming to the Coast.

Back in the day, there were two companies that owned the train. One company, the Quebec Oriental, owned it from New Carlisle to Matapedia and the other company, the Atlantic Québec and Western, owned it from New Carlisle to Gaspé. They used to have a bit of fun with the names, and call them 'Clear Only' and 'All Clear and Wobbly' instead.

The New Carlisle railroad track must have been built around 1900, because the first train to go to Gaspé was in 1910. When they first started to build this track, there was an English company involved, who came here to set up business. They had brought the track as far as Caplan. So they requested that the shareholders advance them more money to bring the train to New Carlisle. The shareholders kind of locked down; they said they weren't going to give them any more money until they brought the track to New Carlisle.

So then the workers here built the New Carlisle station. Not the station they have now, but the previous one, and they took a picture of it. After that, they loaded a locomotive on a scow, brought it to the wharf in New Carlisle and unloaded it. And by then they had the track going from the New Carlisle wharf to the station. So they brought the engine up to the station, took a picture of it sitting in front, and sent it to England saying, 'We have arrived in New Carlisle.'

They got the advance money to bring the track to New Carlisle.

One Car, Two Cars!

As told by Elsie Pye

Elsie was born in the second range of Douglastown in 1904. She married at 18, moved to Sandy Beach and had four children. She was a housewife, caring mother and an active member of the church and Women's Institute. She passed away August 8, 2003, one month shy of her 99th birthday.

You know, when you look back, it's hard to believe how everything has changed since I was little. For one thing my mother always had a basket lying around filled with gingersnaps. And she used to have it hanging up in the pantry because you never knew when someone was going to arrive in the afternoon and stay for tea. She used to keep fruitcake ready in a can, too. Nowadays, you don't go anywhere unless you're invited. And you don't set them down to a cup of tea and some bread and butter and jam and a piece of fruitcake anymore.

We lived on the Second and for us to go to Gaspé from Douglastown where we lived, now that was the same as going to Montreal these days. We sure didn't go every day. Once, I suppose, in the course of the winter. I remember we used to put bricks in the oven, and get them good 'n' hot and put them in the bottom of the sleigh to keep your feet from freezing on the way. We had nice robes to keep us warm, and we would cross the ice over by what used to be the Kennedy place, over to Dan's Point, and up to Haldimand through the shortcut. There wasn't a house through that shortcut.

Then cars came around and I remember one silly game the kids played for amusement. They'd sit on the front doorstep, and one would count the cars going down the road, and the other would count the cars going up the road. I remember one day, they were going to include the colour of the car in the game, but there were too many cars to get the colours. Some kind of a job you'd have to count them now. You'd want about ten people.

Fun in the Ford

As told by Andrew Norton

Andrew was born in Miguasha West in 1913 and wore many hats throughout his working life. He started off as a farmer, but joined the Air Force in 1942. He grew and sold strawberries, had a great garden of plum trees and cut pulp and sold it up until the age of 78. Andrew now resides in Campbellton.

My first car was a 1932 Ford Roadster with a rumble seat and a canvas top. It was a convertible. What colour was it? Well, as Henry Ford said, 'You can get it in any colour you want, just as long as it's black.' That was the colour of my Roadster. I paid $100 for it, that was it. Still, that was a lot of money in those days.

Where did I get it? I had heard that there was a man in Dalhousie who had just enlisted in the Navy and he was looking to sell his car. Well, I had some money saved up from fishing smelt during the winter season, so I decided to go over to Dalhousie to have a look at it. I managed to have $100 in my pocket when I went to see that Ford Roadster.

I went to see the man's wife as he had already left for Halifax. And she was a beautiful woman. I couldn't drive a car at that time – as a matter of fact, I couldn't even drive a wheelbarrow – but I knew it wouldn't take long to learn. I paid her the $100 for the car and then went straight to a garage.

She told me to tell the owner of the garage that I had just bought the car and that it wouldn't stay in second gear. I asked if he could please help me, so he sent one of his men up to get the car and they worked on it all day until they had fixed the problem. Only cost me ten dollars. Then my brother came to meet me after work and he drove the car home.

It was my brother who taught me to drive. I had a hard time learning because the shift was on the floor. It wasn't like the cars today. I had no license and no insurance. I guess we just didn't think about those things in those days. At that time we didn't have a license for anything. Come to think about it, there wasn't even a registration for it.

In the winter of 1942, I learned about a mobile unit of the Air Force in Campbellton, and I decided to enlist. My car was stowed away for the winter, and I wasn't really sure what I should do with it before I left. When I arrived in Lachine for my basic training, I wrote my father and told him to sell it for $85. I could have sold it for $850 at that point, because cars were scarce during the war. But I didn't know what to do with it, so I decided to get rid of it. It sold right away.

My fondest memories of that car are when I would finish my work for the day and then I would be right there to pick up all the girls on the way to the dance. There were very few people who had a car in those days, so mine was a real novelty. I drove that car all summer long. We had so much fun with the rumble seat up and the top down. There were beautiful evenings out under the moonlit sky. I had some great times in that car.

The Wonder of Work

Beavers Don't Need Chainsaws!

As told by Wesley Harrison

Wesley was born 'up the Nor'west' in 1916 and his wife Lois was born in Cascapedia in 1921. Wesley was well-known for his storytelling skills and knowledge about the Cascapedia River. He had a beautiful singing voice and he and Lois often entertained friends with their musical talents. Wesley passed away in 2005.

Wesley Harrison with his pelts

I was just a young fellow of ten years of age when I remember my mother saying that it was time for me to accompany my father in the woods trappin'. She did not like the fact that he would be two weeks alone out in the woods without anyone around to look out for him. The woods can be a dangerous place for a fella on his own. If anything ever happened back there in the woods, he would be in bad shape! My daddy would go 50 miles back into the woods – that's right – 50 miles on foot into the woods. So after I had done about three years of school, I quit and headed into the woods with my daddy.

I kept him company while he was trappin' and helped him carry the pelts on our backs, and stuff like that. We'd be gone two weeks at a time, so we would make a smoke hole to sleep in. That's when you build lumber four feet high and have a fire inside to keep warm, during the cold January and February nights. The wind would be howlin' and the snow would really be coming down. One time I had to chop wood right through the night because I didn't want to freeze to death. A man could easily freeze in there! One night it was forty below zero and, my dear, if I turned to the side of the fire my front almost burned, but at the same time my back almost froze! You were either on fire or you were freezin'. What a life! I told my dad, 'If I gotta do this all the time for a living, then I might as well shoot myself.' He told me not to be so foolish.

We would carry oatmeal and cornmeal and we would catch fish in the lakes for food. It wasn't the lap of luxury. It was just the kind of stuff that kept us going. Then when the trappin' started we had to carry all of those furs on our backs. Sometimes they would be really heavy by the time we got back home, as we had several weeks worth of pelts.

Some of my fondest memories are of trappin' beavers. They are real smart animals, you know.

Back in 1956, the beaver had been over-trapped on the Mingan River, which is on the other side of the St. Lawrence. So the government was giving out contracts for us to trap live beavers at $20 a piece to take them back up to the North Shore and replenish the stock. I spent a few years just doing that. One year I trapped 270 beavers. I used to capture them alive and then they would come here to get them and take them to the airplane. They'd fly them up to Mingan River and drop them off from seaplanes into the lakes and rivers.

I had a proper trap to catch them in. But I caught 26 by the tail as well. My wife would come with me and we'd head out at night and stand on the riverbank, listening for a beaver to come out of his house. Out he would come and swim around the house to make sure that there was no danger. Then he'd go back in, and after ten minutes or so, come back out and pound his tail on the water. If there were still no signs of danger, he'd go back in and get the whole family.

They'd all come out and stand in water about eight inches deep and wash their faces and the rest of their little bodies. We used to keep quiet then, because that is the way to find out how many were in the house. So we would watch the beaver pretty sharply and then we'd grab him by the tail and pull him out of the water. If you weren't fast enough, they would try to bite your arms. We would grab them real quick and put them in the cage. It's a pretty tricky job, but if you needed extra money, you did it.

One time we tore a house apart just to see how it was made. What we found out was that it is made of earth, hay and wood, and that they each have a bedroom. That is how you can tell how many live in the house.

When you really stop to think about it, it's amazing how they can dam those streams and make those treetops fall right in the water. And they don't have chainsaws or anything like that.

An old trapper once told me that the mother only keeps two babies. If she has a third one, she gets rid of it and sure enough, I have trapped lots of beaver all my life and I never found more than two babies with the mother. Nobody knows why, I guess it's some kind of mystery. The two babies grow pretty fast. They stay with the mother about a year and then they go and dam up a little creek of their own.

One time I was up in northern Ontario and this fellow said to me, 'You fellas, do you have many lakes down there?'

I said, 'No, we don't have many lakes, but I know what causes all your lakes up here, it's the beavers. Every little creek I see up here has a beaver dam. And one little dam can bring the water up a foot or two and then the next year another beaver builds a second dam and here you have a dam up four, five or six feet high. And then soon enough you've got your lake. The beavers make all the lakes for you fellas. It's all because of the beavers.'

I once told an architect that if he ever wanted to learn anything about building, all he had to do was watch the beavers building their houses, 'cause they know how to do it right. I remember one time we were driving wood down the Cascapedia River and we had a call from the guy who was waiting on the wood. He said that he hadn't got any wood and he wanted to know why we weren't working. Well, we told him we'd been driving for four or five days, but there was still no lumber coming out. Turns out a beaver had that creek dammed up solid. Those engineers would have to have big construction outfits to dam the creek the way the beavers had done it.

We blew the dam apart with dynamite and in two days time they had closed her again! We had to blow her the next time and dig the beaver out from under her. Imagine that! So I always tell these engineers, take a lesson from those there beavers. They can dam any place they want and they don't even have chainsaws.

An Independent Woman

As told by Elizabeth Mae Budd

Born in 1914 in New Richmond, Mae went to Macdonald College to become a teacher. After working in several different fields, Mae spent many years working on the Cascapedia River. She still resides in New Richmond and at 91 years young, her dynamism is an inspiration to all.

My father was Steve McWhirter and he worked hard to make ends meet. He started off working in Ontario when

Steve McWhirter with daughters Madge, Wona, Mae and Lila in 1920's

they were building the railroad, but came back home to work on the Little Cascapedia River taking care of fishermen. He was also a trapper in the winters. He would go many, many miles into the woods by snowshoe, all by himself, trapping any kind of animal he could get his hands on – beaver, muskrat and fox – whatever he caught in the traps. He would go up there just after Christmas and spend most of the winter there. He'd build himself a little camp in the woods with a bunk and a sleeping bag. There's now a mountain that bears his name in the park, Mount McWhirter.

When he'd come home after a long winter, he'd sell the skins he caught. Then the first thing he'd do is go to the store and buy a barrel of flour, bags of white and brown sugar, beans, all the essentials while he still had the money. It was a tough life. My mother was a seamstress and she made all of our clothes. There were six of us children – I had three sisters and two half-brothers. We would help out with the chores, doing things like helping in the garden and cutting ice for the icebox. There was always something that had to be done. We kept a pig, chickens and a horse. We were truly self-sufficient. My mother made all her own soap as well – lye soap. All year long she would collect bits of fat and rinds and when she made soap, she made enough to last the whole year. She would boil everything in a big pot on our wood stove. That lye soap was very, very white. It was strong too; so you had to be careful making it.

I've worked all of my life as well and I've never really given it a second thought; I just did. I was a teacher, taught grades 1 to 7. One year, I had 45 students to look after. It wasn't easy, let me tell you!

I didn't spend my whole life teaching; I've also worked in offices doing payroll, bills and general office work. I even had a job working on an assembly line with other girls, at a place where they built bombs in Ajax. That was when Ajax had just been born; there wasn't a town there yet.

Eventually, we moved back home and I worked in the salmon fishing camps on the Grand Cascapedia. I worked with my father at one of the camps for seventeen years, doing mostly accounting. My son used to come to work with me when he was small.

I guess you could say I was an 'independent' woman for the time. I remember telling my husband that he had to do his own laundry or find someone to do it, because I was working, too! I worked right up until the time I turned 65 years old and enjoyed it, because I got out of the house and I got to meet interesting people all the time, especially the people back in the camps on the Cascapedia.

The people at these camps were unique and so were the creatures. I've seen bears come out in the evening, open the icehouse door, and steal the ham or baloney. And no matter what you did to scare them, they wouldn't move, they'd just stand there and look at you.

After my mother died, my father would still keep busy by reading and writing. He wrote poems, letters, articles for newspapers and other things. He put together a book of his work, using his own life and experiences for inspiration. This is one of his poems he wrote about our family:

'My Family' – Steve McWhirter
Thanks be to God who has made me
The happiest man on this earth
The father of four lovely children
In my heart there is nothing but mirth.
They have grown now to be women
And families they also now have
But to me they are still my children
And their thoughts are always of Dad.
If their mother was only now seeing
The pleasure her daughters now be
To the man she chose for their father
And how happy the family she would see.
The happiest man now on this earth
Is the one she left alone
The father of her four children
She was the best mother that ever was known.

Trying Times on the Telephone

As told by Elizabeth Robertson Leblanc

Born June 8, 1919 in New Richmond, Elizabeth started working as a telephone receptionist at age 17. She also worked at the New Richmond mill for 14 years. She remains in New Richmond where she enjoys painting as her pastime.

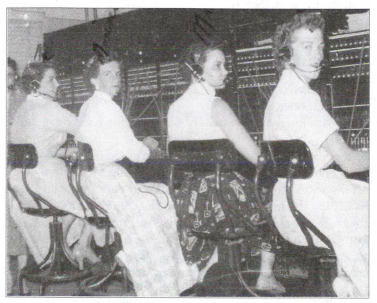

Switchboard Operators in New Carlisle

The Telephone Company of Bonaventure and Gaspé Limited was founded around 1906 by John Hall Kelly from New Carlisle. In the beginning, customers would have to pay for service six months in advance to have a phone installed in their house. Every month, installers would visit them and pick up the money for the long distance calls made. A horse was leased at a dollar a day just so that the installers could make their rounds. The company eventually bought their first service vehicle around 1910. The phone service and switchboard were initially set up in private homes rather than in commercial buildings.

My personal experience with the telephone company began when I was only 17 years old. It was 1936 and I had just finished school. I don't remember whether I had received my teaching diploma or not at that point. It was then that I was offered the position of telephone operator. Mrs. Ida Henderson came to my house and asked me if I'd be interested in working for the phone company because I was bilingual and one of her operators had recently quit. I think I would have preferred to teach, but I could not afford to turn down the money that I was being offered – a big $10 a month – so I accepted. I had to wait until I had worked a full month before I received my first paycheque, but did I ever feel rich when I received that first $10! I was so proud to be making my own money.

My training on the switchboard lasted three days and I learned very quickly how to answer the calls with 'number please.' Since there was no electricity at that time we had to use a crank to ring the numbers. When there was snow or ice on the wires after a storm, the crank was very heavy and hard to handle. I had to learn all the phone numbers by heart, so that when someone called in and asked me to ring someone up, like the garage, I could do it immediately. There was no time to waste. Most of the time, customers just gave me someone's name and expected me to know all the numbers. If I had to look up a number in the directory, the customer was often frustrated and short with me.

We were also expected to know everything that was going on in the community. When the bell rang at church, the phone would immediately start ringing and people would ask who had died. How many calls did I get a day, just to be asked what time of the day it was? And it was exactly the same with the hockey scores. People would call in to find out who had won the hockey match. The hockey season was our busiest time of the winter and God help us if we didn't know the score!

When it came to the phone lines, there were private lines and party lines. Some party lines had up to fifteen customers on them or more. As for long distance calls, there was one line from New Richmond to New Carlisle and then one from

New Richmond to Campbellton. To call any further away, we had to transfer the call. If the operator there was slow, then it could take a very long time to make the long distance call.

There were only two operators at a time working from seven in the morning to eleven at night. In the winter, there was only one operator at a time, but the manager would replace us for breaks or meals and we worked one month on, one month off all winter long. On the days when we weren't really busy, we had plenty of time to read and sew or do other things between calls.

Then electricity started to come in along the Coast during the 1950's and the office was moved and changes began to take place. In 1953, the Telephone Corporation of Quebec acquired the Bonaventure and Gaspé Telephone Company and took over the remainder of the Gaspé Peninsula. Then in 1955, the company constructed a central building in front of the English school in the village. A dial was installed on the switchboard and we were able to signal the three numbers for Maria, Grand Cascapedia and Caplan. Later on, we added the 388 code for Caplan and 759 for Maria. Eventually, Grand Cascapedia took on the same exchange as New Richmond.

I get a bit nostalgic when I recall those times; however, I really appreciate today's communication services like being able to communicate so quickly with my children who live far away. I also like being able to hook into email and be in touch with family and friends from all around the world.

Today we all enjoy the advantages of the modern telephone. My little cordless phone follows me everywhere in the house. Whenever it rings, I remember all the warm voices that I used to speak to when I worked as a telephone operator and the wonderful memories I will treasure always.

The Glass-Eyed Bandit

As told by Mac Sirois

Mac was born in Grand River in 1920 and joined the Army in 1942. He spent most of his life with the Quebec Police Force and after leaving his posting in New Carlisle, he was chief of police in Schefferville for several years. He became a private detective and in 1973 he opened his own security business and subsequently sold it in Seven Islands where he still resides today.

So I arrived in New Carlisle in 1951 to work with a Mr. Traineau who was in charge of the police outpost here. He got sick in April and the department decided that I was going to be in charge; in charge of one man – me. There was nobody else.

The years 1953 and '54 were very busy for me because I had to cover a murder in New Richmond, a bank robbery in Carleton and the Coffin case in Gaspé. The bank robbery in Carleton was a very interesting case: the culprit could not be identified by fingerprints or DNA, 'cause there were no such methods at this time …

The robbery happened on a Wednesday and I was working day and night trying to get a lead. I was getting calls from Campbellton – they had seen a suspicious car; in Matapedia they had seen a suspicious car. I was running all over the place.

Saturday morning rolls around, and with no leads to go on, I go back to Carleton to figure out how they had worked the break-in. I know for a fact that they had worked under what they call a tent. What they do is they come in and put a tent around the safe. There are generally three guys working under it, which was the case in Carleton. There would be one guy keeping watch in the gallery, one cutting the safe and one throwing water – they call him 'la Rousser' in French. So while one guy was cutting the safe with a torch, this other guy was throwing water onto the safe so that the money inside wouldn't burn.

Now, the one who was throwing the water was a guy by the name of Alfred Metayer, who happened to have a glass eye. And this guy, instead of going out the front door of the bank – which is facing the main street, goes out the window and, sweating from the heat under the tent, he loses his glass eye.

When I'm looking around at the bank on Saturday, I happen to look out the window and I see two little boys outside. I see one of 'em picking something up off the ground. So I say to him, 'What have you got there?'

And he says, 'I have a ball.'

'Let me see that ball.' I take the ball and I know right away that it's no ball, it's a glass eye. And I think I've got something there.

I call my boss in Quebec City, Captain Matte, and I tell him I got my big lead, a glass eye. He gives me the names of a few guys who've worked on safes, but we need more information. I stop at the local doctors – Doctor Cavanaugh and Doctor Morin and I ask 'em if it's a right eye or a left eye. Well, they each give me a different answer, so the captain tells me to come up to Quebec to get a specialized opinion. He says, 'In case you have an accident, wrap that eye up well and put it under your spare tire in the trunk.'

Now no one in Quebec City knows anything about the eye, so I go to see a shady character who makes eyes on the side. I find him in a little street and I ask him 'You make eyes?' He looks at the eye and he says, 'I'll tell you something. It's not been made in Quebec City. There's nobody here who can make an eye like that. That's a perfect eye.' He tells me that there's a couple of guys in Montreal who are good at making glass eyes.

I go up to Montreal and I meet with some of the guys, but nobody knows anything about it until I meet up with a Doctor Ross. Then, I take out the glass eye and ask him if he made it. And he says 'Yes.'

'Who did you make this eye for?' I ask him, 'because I'd like to give it back to him.'

He gives me the name of a Mr. LaRousshe, a contractor from Temiscamingue. Now, I had some pictures of possible culprits with me and I pull them out and ask him to ID this Mr. LaRousshe and he points out Metayer.

So, we find out that Metayer, otherwise known as 'The Eye', is in town at the bus terminal buying two tickets for a bus that leaves around 3 pm to go up to Chicoutimi. We pick him up at the bus station. The whole time he keeps saying that no, he had nothing to do with the bank robbery, that he had never even been to Carleton.

However, Metayer was also involved in other cases in Quebec. He's out on bail in Chicoutimi, in Drummondville and in Three Rivers. When we get back to Carleton and prove he'd been there with his glass eye he says, 'Okay. What I'll do is I'll go around to all of the towns with you and I'll plead guilty on all of my cases as long as I don't get more than two years for each.'

'No problem,' I tell him. 'As long as you plead your case, you'll only get two years.'

So we go around to Chicoutimi and all of the other towns. Every time we arrive in a town, I take him to the jail and then find a hotel to stay in overnight before taking him to see the judge in the morning. Each time he pleads guilty they give me his bail money – a thousand dollars, two thousand dollars – it all comes to me and I keep track of it. Now of course we were on the swing, so we don't have time to wash our clothes. We buy clothes as we go. I get pretty friendly with him, as a matter of fact. He's not a violent guy, but he's very, very smooth and very, very intelligent.

We arrive here in New Carlisle and I have the envelope with all of the money and he says to me, 'That money, I won't need it, so I want my mother to get it.' His mother is a very old woman because he's 45 or 47.

I put him in jail and I go see the judge and I say 'I have Metayer here, what are you going to give him?'

And he says 'What should I give him?'

I say, 'Well, he could plead guilty to only seven years, because otherwise it would be a long case that would cost a lot of money.'

'Okay, okay, seven years.' he says.

I go to Alfred and I ask him if he would take seven years, and he says he will. I tell him not to get too excited, but I talked to the judge and all those two-year terms you got from your other cases will be packed in with the seven years. And he says okay.

Now there's another case down the road and two or three guys from Quebec City are there working on it. They all happen to come into New Carlisle the same night that I arrive with Metayer. They're at the Maison Blanche and the honourable judge is there too. They all have a drink together and they convince the judge that Alfred is a very bad man and that he should get 21 years.

I go in the following morning and the judge is in bad shape. It's the morning of Metayer's hearing. The judge says to me, 'That bandit that you brought in, he's not getting his seven years.'

'No?' I say, 'What is he getting then?' He says 21 years. Well I say to him, 'That's not what you told me yesterday. I told you Metayer was pleading guilty for seven years, not 21 years!'

But the judge only says, 'He's getting 21 years!'

So I answer, 'Well then he's not pleading guilty anymore, forget about that!' and I go downstairs to tell Metayer.

I say to him, 'Alfred, I've got very bad news for you – they're giving you 21 years.' And I tell him not to plead guilty. I take him out of the cell for his hearing and we go in the hall and start up the stairs because that's where the court is.

But suddenly he stops me and says, 'I'm going for it. I'm pleading guilty.'

'What do you mean?' I ask him, 'I promised you seven years! If you want seven years, plead not guilty!'

He looks at me and says 'I'm fed up with it, I'm pleading guilty.' So he does, he pleads guilty. He gets 21 years and I am very disappointed because I gave him my word. He tells that judge that he'll take his sentence, but he wants me to take him up to the penitentiary in Montreal.

Well now, I'm a little nervous about why he wants me to take him up. I think to myself, 'Maybe he knows I'm soft on him and he's going to try and make a break for it.' The judge asks me what I think and I say I'll do it.

During the trip I try many ways to get him to talk, but the only way I can get anything from him is to talk about his mother. And if I talk about his mother, the guy cries; 21 years is a long time to be away from family. So he looks at me and asks, 'You'll get the money to my mother?'

I said, 'Yes, of course. Do you want to see your mother?' And then he cries! I cry, too. 'Well,' I said, 'we're going to fix it up. Your mother is an old woman and you're going to be gone for 21 years. You've got no brothers, no sisters, so we'll go and fix up the funeral costs for your mother – we've got the money from your bail. So, no handcuffs and you give me your word you're not going to try anything, because I will be very sorry if I have to shoot you.' He is very happy about going to see his mother.

So he meets his mother, I go in with him to help break the ice. He introduces me as his boss. His mother asks him what he was doing now, and he tells her that he's selling stockings. This is a very good lie. But then he says, 'They find me so good at selling stockings that they're sending me out west to do it. I'm going to be in charge of a group.'

His mother says that out west they speak English, and he says, 'Well, I'll learn.' Then he tells her that he's been making good and he hands the envelope of money to her. After that I go out and leave them alone, because I know that this is the last time he will ever see his mother.

When we get to Mont Joli I say to Alfred, 'I think I'll buy a treat for you.' Throughout our long journey together he had said quite a few times, 'You should buy me a little drink.' And I always said, 'No, I can't do that.' So in Mont Joli I tell him I'll get him a treat and when he asks me what it is, I tell him it's five pairs of socks. I go in and buy him ten ounces of gin, and he signs a receipt for the five pairs of socks instead, so that no one knows the difference.

He died a couple of years later in the penitentiary. I can talk about it now, because everyone is dead. This is a story that I kept to myself while they were living because it was my case and that's what you did with your cases, you kept them.

THE RADIO

The Lone Ranger

As told by Rene Morris

Born in Little Pabos in 1932, Rene worked for 25 years as a millwright at New Richmond Mill. He enjoys hunting, fishing and spends most of his time in his woodworking shop in Pabos Mills.

Our home was the gathering place in the community. We were one of the first ones in Little Pabos to have a radio. I remember when the Lone Ranger would come on. My grandfather, who was in his eighties at the time, would come and find us to let us know that the program would be on shortly. There would be seven or eight of us in the living room listening to the Lone Ranger. When the story came on, no one was allowed to make a sound. Everyone was sitting around and Mamma would be knitting. Afterwards she'd make a nice raisin pie for us to enjoy.

Often when the Lone Ranger was over we would play cards for apples. Especially, in the fall of the year, when the apples were ripe, we would get together and play cards by the hour for an apple.

Two-Radio Town
As told by Lionel Gilker

The radio was our biggest entertainment. I can remember when there were probably only two radios in New Carlisle. We didn't have electrical power back then – the radios were all battery-operated. All the boys would get together on Friday or Saturday night to listen to the Toronto hockey game.

Not many people had radios, probably because they couldn't afford them. They would have been about a hundred dollars or so. A hundred dollars at that time was a lot of money. For some people it was probably a year's salary. And the batteries were a problem too, because they were either car batteries or dry cell batteries. If the radio worked on a car battery, then you could charge it, but if it only ran on drycell you had to buy new ones all the time. So when someone had a radio, well, everybody would congregate!

My Hometown

A Sense of Community

As told by Louis Brochet

My fondest memories of living on Bonaventure Island are the beautiful beaches. Bonaventure Island has some of the most beautiful beaches I have ever seen. I remember when I was a child I was told to stay away from the cliffs, as they were very, very steep and my aunt and uncle were afraid that I might fall off or that something terrible might happen to me. They were very protective of me.

It was like this: I was my mother's seventh child and she died in childbirth of the Spanish Flu. She was only 32 years old. My father already had six children at home to care for, so the family decided it would be best if I was to leave the mainland and go live with my aunt and uncle on Bonaventure Island.

I was not born on the island, but I was raised there and I raised my own family there as well. When I was growing up, there were only eight families living on the island. I think there were about 50 people in total and everyone was English-speaking. We didn't get to hear any French. Our little world was 100% English.

We had one little schoolhouse where the Protestants and Catholics learned together. I remember a wonderful teacher from Barachois. She was a product of the nuns. At recess, she used to teach us how to square dance. Can you just imagine if the nuns ever found out what she was teaching us? I bet that she would have been out of a job in a hurry. She stands out in my mind because she was so kind and caring with us.

When I was little, I would play in the ponds and brooks with the little boats I made with my own hands. There was a big ridge of rocks behind our house and I remember that I had to be very careful there because it would have been very easy to slip and fall; but it was also a good lookout and I could watch anybody passing up or down the road. It was my private spot. No one knew about it and I could go there and feel as though I was all alone in the world.

In those days, you were either a fisherman or a farmer or both. Preferably both; because that was the only way to make any kind of a living. Everybody had nine or ten head of cattle; half a dozen to a dozen sheep; hens and pigs – everything it took. We would kill a pig in the fall and salt it for the winter, because there were no refrigerators in those days.

In late October of every year, my uncle would kill a pig and he would take a piece to each neighbour. Each family on the island did this, so in the fall we were always guaranteed some fresh meat. Then my uncle would salt the pork to keep it for the winter. Back then, neighbours looked out for one another.

If a farmer needed a new barn, everyone on the island helped him to build it. No one thought twice about who he was or whether they should help or not, they just did it. That's the way it was growing up on the island. We all helped one another survive. If one family was going through difficult times, we'd all be there to lend a helping hand. I believe we were much closer as a community because we were so isolated. We had to rely on one another.

I used to fish lobster on Bonaventure Island as a kid – about 15 or 16 years old. I fished lobster for a cent and a half a pound, so it's a big change from today. We didn't have gasoline motors or anything like that; we just had the old-fashioned poverty sticks – oars, of course. We called them poverty sticks, but they were oars.

Codfish was the same. I fished codfish for a little better than half a cent a pound. That was for fish under 23 inches long. It wasn't a question of making money; it was a question of survival more than anything else. By 1942, I was getting four cents a pound, which was considered very good. And twenty or forty bucks a day in 1942 was good money. Can you believe that I left it to go work in the Army for a dollar-thirty a day?

I met my wife on the island. In fact, she was my next-door neighbour. And there's nothing like a Gaspé girl, you see. In the summertime and fall we could take a boat to the mainland. At that time, there was an ice bridge that built up between the island and the mainland for two or three months during the winter. It took a combination of correct temperatures, tides and winds for the ice bridge to develop and it would only harden once every three or four years. Sometimes, we would be stuck for weeks before the ice bridge would be hard enough for us to travel over it. Those days proved to be very long.

Well, the last year that I was there, I was caught in the water for over four hours and then had to stay on the mainland overnight before I could return to my family. When I returned after that disaster, I told my wife that I had decided that we had had enough of island living and it was time for us to move to the mainland. She agreed and that spring we moved.

It was a big adjustment for us, but you know there are good and bad in all things. On the mainland, the children learned to speak French and English, something that is a real gift. They did not have this opportunity on the island because the island was only English-speaking. On the other hand; on the island, we had a close-knit community, something we never really experienced again on the mainland.

Hobos and Bootleggers

As told by Ethelyn Vautier and Orva Vautier

Ethelyn was born in 1919 in Bromont and was a well-respected school teacher all her life. She also shared the responsibilities of running a fishing supplies shop with her husband in Shigawake, where she still resides. Orva was born in Shigawake in 1924 and worked as a telephone receptionist and at Gaspé hospital during wartime. Orva married a boy in the Air Force and spent several years in England. She now resides in North Hatley where she enjoys her evening phone calls from her sister-in-law and former neighbour, Ethelyn.

You don't see many hobos around the Coast today, but when I was a young girl, there were plenty of them in Shigawake. They would carry a stick with a bag tied to the end of it, just like they do in the movies; filled with clothing or something to eat. The hobos would travel back and forth along the Coast, some by train, and others by foot. Most of them would 'ride the rails' as they say. This meant that they would hitch a ride on the train, hiding either underneath or on top and even inside the boxcars. The hobos that we saw traveled the roads. They'd get hungry and come into town looking for food.

My father died when I was only three, but that never changed my mother's generosity. She was left with four children to bring up on her own with no income to speak of, but she would always give the hobos her last bowl of soup.

We used to have a gallery that went right around the house, so they'd just put down their sack, stretch out right there and go to sleep. We didn't know who these people were but they would come and spend the night at our house! It was just the right thing to do in those days.

To be honest, the hobos weren't the only strangers prowling our quiet neighbourhood, there also happened to be a lot of bootleggers around. Most of the bootlegging happened on a clear moonlit night. My mother would hush us all up in bed before a car would come up the road and secretly park behind the house. She would whisper 'Don't make any noise. Say your prayers and go to bed.'

The police would be driving back and forth along the road looking for the bootlegger and he'd be parked behind our house hiding from them the whole time. My mother was a widow so they never thought to look around our house. Once they had gotten tired of looking for him, they'd drive away and he'd escape. We all knew he was from Douglastown and stored his liquor in our lane.

There was another bootlegger from Hopetown who ran a much bigger operation. And then there was this foreign lady who did business with him, she was always dressed to the hilt. A lady bootlegger – what a clever idea. Who would ever suspect? She was an American and she came all the way to the Gaspé Coast to pick up liquor that came in by boat. They would fill her car with moonshine and liquor and she always managed to cross the border without suspicion.

Douglastown seemed to have its share of bootleggers, because there was another fellow from the area who knew when the shipments were coming in on the boats, and he'd be there to pick up the liquor. He knew the police were never far behind, so he had to be careful. He'd tie his rowboat to the big transport ship, keeping well out of sight from the dock. No one ever knew that he was unloading liquor from the other side of the ship! The ship would set sail with the liquor-filled rowboat still attached. When the ship passed Gascons, the smaller boat would be released.

As the police were always looking for him, he would sail out to the Newport Isles and light a lantern, placing it on a rock where it would be sure to attract attention. The police would see the light, and get into a boat to sail out to the island to investigate a possible bootlegging. And while they were busy investigating, the bootlegger had the time he needed to unload the liquor into a car he'd have waiting near the bridge in Gascons. He'd be long gone by the time the police realized it was only a lantern. Tricks of the trade, you know.

York of Yesteryear

As told by Francis Annett

Francis was born in Gaspé in 1901. He was known for his photographic memory, and when a fire took place at the Howard Smith Pulp and Paper office, he amazingly recited, from memory, the missing information from files which were destroyed. He loved to play cards, travel and listen to music. Francis passed away in 1998.

We grew up right here in York. Oh yes, there was a number of us boys grew up here together. The Stewart boys and the Jones boys.

As young fellows in the summertime, we spent a lot of our time in the water, down there on the shores of York River. York Bay you might call it. Swimming and wading and playing down on the beach. Then we used to do work with our mother and father – sometimes a little in the garden, haymaking would come up and milking and stable work. Hunting and fishing too, every boy did that.

When we were a little older we used to have house dances. It was fun but so hot with all those people packed into one room. I don't think you ever opened a window in those days! Those dances were a big time. And fiddlers – oh, there was all kinds of fiddlers here in York! We were polluted with fiddlers! There was the Stewart family and three or four of them that played the violin. Of course, that was the only piece of instrument other than the organ. But the organ, you didn't move that from house to house.

I went to school here in York to grade 7 and then went up to grade 10 in Gaspé. After school I got my first job with a scaler in the woods. 'Tallyman,' they used to call it. I tallied the scales, don't think we made much more than a dollar a day. After that I did clerical work for the Howard Smith paper mill. They were in the pulpwood business, and they'd cut the lumber up on one of the three rivers – the York, the Dartmouth or the St. Jean. They drove it down in the spring of the year and towed it down to the mill in Sandy Beach. And they'd come out with four-foot length logs, put a steel drum around them and ship them off to Ontario from the Sandy Beach wharf.

Then I got an auditing permit in 1931. Now previously, anyone who could add two and two together would be appointed as an auditor. But the government wanted more than that. So they had a little course in it. It was held in Percé.

I ended up doing the auditing for the municipalities and schools. Now there was another man, a Mr. Leo Kennedy, and he had a permit in Douglastown. But between him and I, we did all the districts around. They weren't very big budgets compared to today. No comparison, my dear, no comparison.

Then I became secretary-treasurer of York. Mr. Dan Price was the secretary and he died, so they appointed me as secretary-treasurer. I was still secretary-treasurer when the big amalgamation came with the Town of Gaspé in 1970. Well, I didn't think too much of it, to be frank about it.

Good honest people, who didn't have that much money, were frightened that the taxes would go much higher. Oh my God almighty! I was paying around $75 to $100 and today I'm paying close to $1,500. I don't know, to be honest, if we got much more to show for it.

Now I was involved in the evaluations process as well and the evaluators had to go from house to house. Years ago you would go to people's houses and say, 'Yes you've got a nice house, and it's big. Oh my,' I'd say, 'you're valued at $2,000, but I think we'll put you up to $2,500.' That was it, away you went. But then the council demanded that we measure every building! So that was a lot of work. There must have been twenty of us on it. We did it from Fox River to Barachois. That's a big district.

Gaspé was a busy village. There was Robin Jones which we used to call CRC – Collis, Robin, and Collis. Most of their staff was from the island of Jersey. They were a big outfit, Robin Jones. They used to have stores right out on the end of the wharf.

Steamships like the *S.S. Gaspesia* and *The North Gaspé* would come in and onload their passengers. They would run between Montreal and Gaspé and over to Newfoundland, and then back to Gaspé and pick up the passengers from freight or express and go back to Montreal.

There was no bridge here in those days. It was all by ferry and they used to run with a scow. They'd tow the scow over and then take back the horses. Then the bridge was built and the official opening was in 1934. Oh my, but it saved people time. That was a big undertaking. They had a bad accident there too. There was one or two men drowned.

During World War II, I was a busy young man in Gaspé. Oh my God man! I don't know how to explain it to you. There was so many young people who went in the Army. They nearly cleaned Gaspé out! Some places, three and four of them from one house. It was awful. There was so many of our friends gone – there was so much sadness.

Now you see, they used to have this base in Sandy Beach as a naval base. And they also had an air base too. Oh yes, there was a lot of planes. We had a lot of young men here from other places, too. Oh there was an awful pile. Those boats used to come in with probably thousands of them on those big boats. Hadn't been ashore for probably a month or so, or a couple months. There was a lot of boats sank out there too off Cap des Rosiers. I know different times they brought in boatloads from Cap des Rosiers and Fox River that had been rescued.

We had a blackout here in Gaspé during the war, no lights allowed. And, oh yes, there was rationing, we had to get cards. And no sugar! Not too many treats, we had to be an inventive bunch.

I believe my brother James had one of the first radios in York. We used to go over there and they used to have generally one or two sets of earphones, as they called them. You put them on your ears. And if there were any more than two or four to listen, we used to take the receiver off the telephone and screw that on the earphone and then we could listen with one ear.

I was involved on the first board for bringing the television in here with Mr. Wilfred Carter and Mr. Fred Vibert. It was an awful lot of work. It came on the air I think in September

1962. There were problems with that mountain. We had to get all that equipment up to the top of that mountain! Oh my God, that was a big change! Getting in touch with the outside world.

Now, my daughter and her family are living with me and we get an awful lot of joy out of living with our grandchildren and watching them grow up and helping them, telling them the ways and means of life. Don't worry, they teach us plenty, too! A lot of happiness.

The Bridge

Aurora Patterson Drainville, Age 6, Belle Anse Elementary School

Once upon a time when my Nana was young there was no bridge in Gaspé. In winter, people crossed on the ice, but that is another story.

In summer, people crossed the river by ferryboat. By the wharf was a little house. In the house was a bench to sit on and a bell to ring. If the ferry was not there you had to ring a bell and the ferry would come across the river and get you. At night it was dark and sometimes it was cold. After we crossed the river we had to climb very big stairs. It was a lot of walking for a little girl.

In 1934, a bridge was built. It was very exciting. Everybody went out to walk on the new bridge.

Growing up in Douglastown

As told by Lorna Holland

Lorna was born in Douglastown in 1926 and after completing grade 10, started teaching in Seal Cove when she was just 16. She married William Holland and they had seven children together. After living in Montreal for twenty years, they retired to the Gaspé.

We may not have had much as kids growing up in Douglastown, but the one thing we did have was a lot of fun.

We used to play cards and board games, but the highlight of our days was going to the post office. We kids always used to hang out at the post office. I will never forget Mr. Kennedy, the postmaster we had for years and years. He was as nasty as anything; mad as a rooster. We would all go there together on our bicycles. Sometimes the boys would take us girls on their handlebars. That was always so much fun. We would go all over the place on the bikes.

After school, we would come rushing home to listen to the radio. There was one program in particular that I remember, it was called *Pepper Young's Family* and we never missed it. It was like a modern day soap opera. It was all about people getting married and living with one another's wives and getting divorced. Much like the way the world is today.

We didn't have cars, but in the winter we did have the loveliest horses with bells on. We'd go riding on sleighs. It was a lot of fun tearing through the village with the bells on the horses ringing. I especially remember the fun we would have at Christmas time.

I am sure that we believed in Santa Claus until we were 9 or 10 years of age. We would decorate the tree with strings of popcorn, tinsel and a few small balls. I can recall running and tearing down the stairs to find everything under the tree. The presents weren't elaborate, but they were meaningful. Sometimes I would get a nice new pair of mittens or a new slate for school. We were so excited if we got a new slate to take notes on. It was even more exciting when the new ones came out that we could write on and then lift up and they would erase themselves.

That was like magic to us back then.

In school we were taught by the sisters in their own broken English. Unfortunately, we believed everything they told us.

I can remember the chores we had to do and how hard it was, but it never hurt us. We used to pick berries and help with the garden. We did the planting and digging before going to school in the morning. On Saturdays and Sundays, we'd help with the chores in the house before we could go outside and play with our friends.

We spent a lot of time taking moonlight walks on the beach with our boyfriends, playing games and just spending entire evenings there. The most fun of all growing up in

Douglastown was when we used to make bonfires on the beach. We even tortured the local carpenters to let us have lumber for our fires. Sometimes we would build a large platform and talk a fiddler into coming and playing music for us so we could dance under the moonlight on the beach. They are such fond, pleasant memories.

Yes, these are some of my best memories of growing up in Douglastown.

Box Socials

As told by Carl and Ella Gillis

Carl Gillis, born in Gaspé in 1917, is a retired World War II veteran of the 64th Battery of the Royal Canadian Artillery. He owned a pastry shop and a service station in Gaspé. Ella was born in Gaspé in 1922, and worked as a caregiver, as well as a housekeeper. The couple reside in Gaspé and have recently celebrated their 65th wedding anniversary.

When we were teenagers, we'd hang out at the covered bridge in Wakeham. We would sit on the side of the bridge and talk and share chocolate bars. There were always several couples hanging out and sharing jokes or cuddling under the covered bridge. At the end of the night, we'd walk home together. We'd go to the bridge two, maybe three times a week.

Sometimes a car would try to get through the bridge, but there would be so many bikes lined up that it would take them a long time to get through. They would literally have to creep by us to pass. Other times we would sit on the grass beside the bridge and have a bonfire and sing songs. If someone had a mouth organ then we would have a little bit of music, which we all liked a lot. We just talked and laughed and had a good time. That was what our courting days were like under that covered bridge.

We also loved to go to dances. We used to have what we called 'box socials.' We had a box social about two or three times a year in the hall in Wakeham. The girls would make a lunch and put it in a box and take it to the dance. We would

Carl and Ella Gillis with baby Gene

make a sandwich to put in the box, as well as a cookie or two and sometimes an apple. The boys didn't know what girl had made what box and they would buy a box and then had to share it with the girl who had made it. You just had to take a chance. The girls made the boxes and the boys did the buying. The first time Carl and I went to a box social, he took a chance and got my box lunch, and we have been sharing meals ever since.

We knew from the very first time we met, that was it, we both knew. I was a Protestant and he was a Catholic and we got married in Montreal, after going to two different churches to find one willing to marry us. We ended up getting married in the United Church and have been married for 65 years. Oh, we've had our ups and downs, but we forget about them and remember only the good times. And it all started with a box social.

Index of contributors

Index